MW00640090

1298

Speaking
Of Christmas

Plays For
Readers' Theater

Matthew Powell, O.P.

CSS Publishing Company, Inc., Lima, Ohio

SPEAKING OF CHRISTMAS

For more information about CSS Publishing Company resources, visit our website at www.csspub.com or e-mail us at custserv@csspub.com or call (800) 241-4056.

ISBN 0-7880-2333-0   PRINTED IN U.S.A.

*In memory of my former students
who have died:*

*Christine Venice Beyer
David Dobbins
Beau Koch
Charles Koon
Gregory Paredes*

and any others I do not know about.

May they rest in peace.

Table Of Contents

A Thousand Years Of Christmas Plays

The Christmas play is a 1,000-year-old tradition in the Christian church. The earliest known Christmas play, the *Officium Pastorum* or Office of the Shepherds, dates from the eleventh century. It was only a short, formal piece performed in Latin by the clergy during Christmas Matins (morning prayer). Apparently, a veiled picture of the Virgin Mary and the Infant Jesus was placed on the altar. Two groups of clerics, representing the shepherds and the midwives (who helped to deliver the baby Jesus), entered from opposite doors and processed to the altar. A boy dressed as an angel greeted them by singing, "Glad tidings" and "Whom do you seek in the manger?" The "shepherds" and "midwives" responded, "We seek Jesus our Lord, a child wrapped in swaddling clothes." The "angel" pointed to the altar and pulled back the veil from the picture of Mary and the Infant. The "shepherds" and "midwives" then sang a threefold alleluia.

It was hardly a great spectacle, but the Christmas play had been born.

The custom spread throughout Europe, plays became more elaborate and were eventually performed in the vernacular and by the laity. Fictional characters and comic elements eventually made their way into the performances. In *The Second Shepherds' Play*, performed in Wakefield, England, the antics of a rogue trying to pass a stolen lamb off as a baby delighted the audience. In a French mystery play, the actors even portrayed the animals in the stable. The cock crowed, *"Christus natus est"* (Christ is born). The ox mooed *"Ubi."* The lamb answered, "Bethlehem," and the donkey brayed, *"Eamus!"* (Let us go). After plays about the crucifixion of Jesus, Nativity plays became the most popular religious plays in Medieval Europe.

Epiphany or Magi plays developed from the Nativity plays and the character of King Herod, usually portrayed as a raging maniac, became a favorite with audiences. In fact, the playing of the part of Herod became so associated with bombastic acting, that Shakespeare used it as a warning against over-acting in the advise to the players in *Hamlet*. He has Hamlet state, "It out-herods Herod. Pray you avoid it."

The ceremony that Saint Francis of Assisi performed in the Italian village of Greccio, which is often credited with being the first Christmas crèche, was actually in the tradition of the Nativity play. Francis got an ox, a donkey, a manger, and either a real baby or a doll (the text is unclear), and used them as a living illustration while he preached to the assembled people.

The Protestant Reformation brought an end to much of the religious drama of Europe because Catholics and Protestants could not agree on the theological content of many of the plays. However, the Christmas play survived because the Incarnation, that God the Son became a man in the person of Jesus Christ, is central to Christianity and was something that all Christians embraced. In addition, Christmas plays followed naturally from belief in the Incarnation. God first became visible to human eyes and audible to human ears with the birth of Jesus to the Virgin Mary in Bethlehem. How appropriate, then, to observe and celebrate that event with something that people could see and hear.

German Catholics and Lutherans both observed a custom called *Kindelwiegen* (Rocking the Child) in which the pastor would carry in a cradle containing a statue of the Infant Jesus and place it on or near the altar. The cradle was then rocked while the congregation sang lullaby-like carols.

Spanish missionaries brought the first Christmas plays to the Americas. Those plays still survive in two Hispanic customs. One is *Las Posadas* (The Inns), a combination outdoor drama and prayer service in which actors representing Mary (sometimes on a donkey) and Joseph go from house to house in the neighborhood in the days before Christmas. They are followed by members of the community who sing and recite prayers along the way. Mary and Joseph are rejected at several houses and finally accepted at a house, where more prayers are recited and Mary, Joseph, and the others are invited in for a celebration with food and dancing.

The other is *Los Pastores* (The Shepherds), a more formal play. Usually performed in a civic lodge or church hall, it is a direct descendant of the Spanish Medieval plays. In the play, angels announce the birth of the Savior to the shepherds, who then begin their journey to Bethlehem. However, the devils do their best to stop the shepherds. This is where improvisation and comic relief enter into the play, with the devils sometimes "threatening" audience members with their pitchforks. Eventually, of course, the devils are vanquished and the shepherds arrive at the stable to worship the newborn Savior.

The twentieth century saw the development of more secular Christmas plays. However, even many Christmas entertainments which are not overtly religious still subtly continue the message of the herald angels — peace on earth, good will to all.

Such plays can be a new way of re-telling an old truth. An example of this is the dramatization of Charles Dickens' *A Christmas Carol* which has become a seasonal staple of regional theaters across the U.S. and Canada. Even though audiences know the story of Ebenezer Scrooge by heart, they return to see it year after year to be reminded of the important values of charity, kindness, and love of fellow man.

Whether it is an improvised street pageant, a play in a church hall performed by children, a spectacle performed in a theater, or a staged reading like those contained in this book, the Christmas play continues to remind us that we give to one another during this season because God gave his greatest gift to us.

What Is Readers' Theater?

Readers' theater is a hybrid form that may be as old as Hrosvitha of Gandersheim, the first woman playwright and a tenth-century German Benedictine nun who wrote plays to be done as staged readings by the sisters in her abbey. Readers' theater is a cross between storytelling and a full theatrical production. For the actor it means *suggesting* a character rather than *becoming* it. It allows the actor to portray a much older person, someone of the opposite gender, an animal, or the North Wind without the benefit of a costume. In readers' theater, a physically disabled person could play an Olympic athlete. For the director, it means ease of production in regard to scenery and costumes. Mountains, cities, and angels' wings are suggested rather than built. For the audience member, it means using the imagination to a greater degree than in a traditional play.

One of the great advantages of readers' theater is that it allows us to perform pieces of literature that, unlike plays, were not originally written to be performed. The plays in this collection are all based on stories or legends that have been adapted for the stage. Their original authors might have intended for them to be read, but these stories can also succeed as performance pieces. Literature was originally a performance as well as a writing art. Poems (intended to be recited out loud) and plays (written to be performed) are the oldest forms of literature. Only the invention of the printing press made the novel and the short story possible. Readers' theater helps us to return to the oral tradition of literature.

In readers' theater the actors traditionally have the script in their hands. This is not because the actors in readers' theater are too lazy to memorize lines. Since readers' theater makes use of a great deal of narration and direct address to the audience, the script serves as a reminder of the *storytelling* aspect of the art form. It emphasizes that the actors, as a group rather than an individual, are reading a story to you and only suggesting the action. They allow the imagination of the audience to do the rest.

11

You might compare readers' theater to being in the studio audience during the golden age of radio drama. Or you might think of it as a story hour for adults.

For information on staging readers' theater consult the following resources:

- *RT: A Readers' Theater Ministry* by Todd V. Lewis (Kansas City: Lillenas Publishing Company, 1988). This short book (46 pages) introduces the inexperienced director to the use of readers' theater in the church setting.
- *Group Reading: Readers' Theatre* by Roy A. Beck (Lincolnwood, Illinois: National Textbook Company, 1985). This 24-page pamphlet takes the reader from locating suitable scripts to final performance.
- *Readers' Theatre — Its Methods and Techniques*, an audio cassette with Marion Furman, Ph.D. (Colorado Springs: Meriwether Publishing, Ltd). Extremely practical, this tape gives the listener the why, what, when, and how of the art form in one hour. See the Appendix in the back of this book for publisher information.

About The Plays In This Volume

This collection contains twelve short plays on Christmas themes suitable for readers' theatre. Playing time varies from only about five minutes to slightly over twenty minutes. The plays can, and should, be performed with a bare minimum of production values (scenery, costumes, and so on) and with the actors using their scripts as a reference during performance. A few chairs, stools, or benches are all the plays need and they can be performed in a church chancel, classroom, or lounge as easily as in an auditorium. Do not make the mistake, however, of thinking that these plays need no rehearsal. While they can be performed well with a minimum of rehearsals, the director should give sufficient attention to the volume, rate, expression, emphasis, phrasing, eye contact, and stage presence of the actors and make sure that they fully understand the text. The stage directions in the plays are only suggestive. The director should feel free to adapt the movement to the space that he or she is using. Readers' theater does not demand an experienced director. If one is available, so much the better. However, anyone who has experience training lectors to read scripture for worship services should also find himself or herself well prepared to stage a reader's theater production. The readers' theater resources previously mentioned should be of great assistance.

These plays are intended for use in a Christian context — worship services, prayer groups, religious education classes, retreats, or as entertainment for parish social events. Five of the plays are specifically religious and four others are, what this writer calls for lack of a better word, inspirational. These inspirational scripts are introduced by Bible quotes that may help in placing the plays to a Christian context. The Bible passages might be spoken by the narrators/storytellers, printed in a program, or disregarded as the director chooses. Three of the plays were added just for fun. Christian groups might enjoy these short humorous pieces and find them useful in their celebration of Christmas.

A Discussion Among Angels

Cast
Storyteller
The Archangel Michael
The Archangel Uriel
The Archangel Raphael
The Archangel Gabriel

(The Storyteller stands off to one side. Michael, Uriel, and Raphael are seated in the center and stand when they speak and remain standing. Gabriel sits slightly farther back from the others. He stands and comes forward when he finally speaks)

Storyteller: A company of angels, returning from their various labors on earth, was sitting in friendly conversation. There were three of the company who seemed to be leaders, distinguished not only by more radiant and powerful looks, but also by a tone of authority in their speech and by the willing attention with which the other angels listened to them, as they talked of their earthly tasks, of the tangles and troubles, the wars and miseries that they had seen among humans, and of the best way to get rid of them and bring sorrow to an end.

Michael: The earth is full of oppression and unrighteousness.

Storyteller: By his shining armor and the long two-handed sword hanging from his shoulder, one knew that the angel speaking was the Archangel Michael, the mightiest of the warriors of God, and the executor of divine punishments on the unjust.

Michael: The earth is tormented with injustice and the great misery that I have seen there is because the evil hand is often stronger than the good hand and can beat it down. The arm of the cruel is heavier than the arm of the kind. The unjust get the better of the

15

just and tread on them. I have seen tyrant kings crush their help-less people. I have seen the fields of the innocent trampled into ruin by the feet of conquering armies. I have seen wicked nations overcome people who loved liberty and take away their freedom by force of arms. I have seen poverty mocked by arrogant wealth, and purity deflowered by brute violence, and gentleness and fair-dealing bruised in the winepress of iniquity and pride.

Michael: *(Pauses thoughtfully)* There is no cure for this evil, ex-cept by giving greater force to the good hand. The righteous cause must be strengthened with sufficient might to resist the wicked, to defend the helpless, to punish all cruelty and unfairness, to uphold right everywhere, and to enforce justice with unconquerable arms. Oh, that the hosts of heaven might be called, arrayed, and sent to mingle in the wars of men, to make good victorious, to destroy evil, and to make the will of God prevail! We would shake down the thrones of tyrants and loosen the bonds of the oppressed! We would hold cruel and violent men with the bit of fear, and drive the greedy and the fierce with the whip of terror! We would stand guard, with weapons drawn, around the innocent, the gentle and the kind, and keep the peace of God with the swords of the angels!

Storyteller: As Michael spoke, his hands were lifted to the hilt of his long blade, and he raised it high above him, throwing out sparks. Then another angel began to speak, and made answer to Michael. He, too, was tall and wore the look of power. But his was the power of the mind rather than of the hand. His great wings, spiral-ing to a point far above his head, were like a living lamp before the altar of the Most High. By this sign, one could tell that this was the archangel Uriel, deepest in wisdom of all the spirits that surround the throne of God.

Uriel: I do not hold the same thought as the great archangel Michael. Nor, though I desire the same end which he desires, would I seek it in the same way. I know how often power has been given to the good, and how often they have turned it aside and used it for evil. I know that the hosts of heaven have fought on the side of a favored nation, yet pride has followed triumph, and oppression has been the first-born child of victory. I know that the liberators of people have sometimes become tyrants over those whom they have set free. I have seen fighters for liberty change into soldiers of fortune. Power corrupts and might cannot save.

Doesn't the Archangel Michael remember how the angel of the Lord led the armies of Israel and gave them victory over every foe ... except the enemy within their own camp? And how the wickedness of the tribes of Canaan survived their conquest and overcame their conquerors, so that the children of Israel learned to worship the idols of their enemies?

Storyteller: There was silence for a moment and then a cool wind brought the sound of chains clanking in prisons and galleys, the sighing of millions of slaves, the weeping of wretched women and children.

Uriel: Power corrupts and might cannot save. The earth is full of ignorant strife, and for this evil there is no cure ... except by giving humans greater knowledge. It is because humans do not understand evil that they yield to its power. Wickedness is folly in action and injustice is the error of the blind. It is because men are ignorant that they destroy one another, and at last themselves.

If there were more light in the world there would be no sorrow. If the great God who knows all things would enlighten the world with wisdom — wisdom to understand his law and his ways, to read the secrets of the earth and the stars, to discern the workings of the human heart, and the things that make for joy and peace — if God would just send us, his messengers, as a flame of enlightenment to shine on those who sit in darkness, how gladly would we go to bring in a new day!

We would speak words of warning and counsel to the erring, and give knowledge to the perplexed. We would guide the ignorant in the paths of prudence.

Then folly would fade away as the morning vapor and rays of wisdom would shine on all people, and the peace of God would come with the counsel of the angels.

Storyteller: A murmur of pleasure followed the words of Uriel and eager looks flashed around the circle of angels as they heard the praise of wisdom. But there was one among them on whose face a shadow of doubt rested. Though he smiled, it was as if he remembered something the others had forgotten.

Raphael: Who was it to whom you were sent to counsel long ago? Was it not Balaam as he was riding his donkey to meet the king of Moab? And did not even the dumb beast profit more from your instruction than the man who rode him? Who was it who was called the wisest of all men, having searched out and understood the many inventions that are found under the sun? But was not Solomon unable by much learning to escape weariness and despair of the spirit? Knowledge also is vanity and vexation. This I know well because I have dwelt among humans and have held conversations with them since the day when I was sent to instruct the first man in Eden.

Storyteller: The others looked more closely at the one who was speaking and recognized the beauty of the Archangel Raphael.

Raphael: Too well I know that power corrupts itself and that knowledge cannot save. There is no cure for the evil that is in the world ... except by giving more love to humans. The ways that are ordained for the earth are strange and unequal and the ways in which men and women walk are full of pitfalls and dangers. Frail is the flesh of humans and many are their pains and troubles. Their children can never find peace until they learn to love one another and help one another.

Wickedness is begotten by disease and misery. Violence comes from poverty and hunger.

The cruelty of oppression is when the strong trample the weak under their feet. The bitterness of pride is when the wise and the learned despise the simple. The crown of folly is when the rich think that they are gods ... and the poor think that God is not.

Hatred, envy, and contempt are the curse of life. For these there is no remedy ... except love — the will to give and to bless, the will of God himself who gives to all and is loving to all.

Raphael: *(Pauses thoughtfully; his mood changes to one of discouragement)* But how can the hearts of humans be won over to the will of love? How will it enter into them and possess them? Even the idols that men fashion for themselves are cruel, proud, and unjust. How will this miracle be brought about in human nature to reveal the meaning of love to humanity? How will men and women become like God himself?

Storyteller: At this question a deep hush fell over the angels. *(Pauses)* Then through the silence, like the song of a far away bird, a voice came ringing.

Gabriel: I know! I know! I know!

Storyteller: Clear as a ray of light, sweeter than the smallest silver bell was that voice.

Gabriel: I know. I know.

Storyteller: All the angels turned to look at the speaker with wondering eyes. Multitudes of others came flying swiftly to the place from which the new voice was sounding.

Gabriel: I know.... Man will be made like God because the Son of God will become a man.

Storyteller: At this all the angels looked at one another with amazement and gathered more closely around the bearer of this astonishing news.

Raphael: How can this be? How is it possible that the Son of God will become a human?

Gabriel: I do not know how. I only know that it is to be.

Michael: But if the Son of God becomes a man, he will be at the mercy of men. The cruel and the wicked will have power over him. He will suffer.

Gabriel: I know. But by suffering he will understand the meaning of all sorrow and pain and he will be able to comfort everyone who cries. His own tears will be for the healing of sad hearts. And those who are healed by him will learn for his sake to be kind to each other.

Uriel: But if the Son of God becomes a true man, he must first be a child, simple, lowly, and helpless. It may be that he will never study at the great universities. The masters of earthly wisdom will despise him and scorn him.

Gabriel: I know that, too. But in meekness he will answer them. And to those who become as little children he will give the heavenly wisdom that comes, without seeking, to the pure and gentle of heart.

Michael: But if he becomes a man, evil men will hate and persecute him. Why, they may even take his life if they are stronger than he!

Gabriel: *(Sadly)* I know. They will nail him to a cross. But when he is lifted up he will draw all people to himself, for he will still be the Son of God. And no heart that is open to love can help but love him since his love for humanity is so great that he is willing to die for them.

Raphael: But how do you know all these things? Who are you?

Gabriel: I am Gabriel. At first, I was sent as the dream of a little child, a holy child to dwell in the heart of a pure virgin, Mary of Nazareth. There I was hidden until the word came to call me back to the throne of God and to give me a new message.

For this is Christmas day on earth and today the Son of God is born of a woman. So I must fly quickly, before the sun rises, to bring the good news to those happy people who have been chosen to receive it.

Storyteller: As he said this, Gabriel rose, with arms outspread, and dropped as swiftly as a shooting star toward the earth. The other angels followed him — a throng of dazzling forms, beautiful as a rain of jewels falling from the dark blue sky. And as they followed him they wondered who had been favored and chosen to receive the glad tidings.

Michael: It must be the emperor and his counselors.

Storyteller: But the flight passed over Rome.

Uriel: It must be the philosophers and masters of learning.

Storyteller: But the flight passed over Athens.

Raphael: It must be the high priest, and the scribes and elders.

Storyteller: But the flight passed over Jerusalem. It floated out over the hill country of Bethlehem. The village was still, the very houses seemed asleep. But in one place there was a low sound of singing in a stable, near to an inn, the sound of a mother soothing her baby to rest. All over the pastures on the hillsides a light film of snow had fallen. As Gabriel passed over them, the fields sparked around him, giving back his radiance.

And there were in that country shepherds abiding in the fields, keeping watch over their flocks by night. And lo! the angel of the Lord came upon them, and the glory of the Lord shone round them, and they were sore afraid. And the angel said unto them:

Gabriel: Fear not, for behold I bring you glad tidings of great joy which shall be to all nations. For unto you is born this day in the city of David, a Savior, which is Christ the Lord. And this shall be a sign unto you, you shall find the babe wrapped in swaddling clothes, lying in a manger.

Storyteller: And suddenly there was with the angel a multitude of the heavenly hosts, praising God and saying,

21

Michael, Uriel, Raphael, and Gabriel: Glory to God in the highest, and on earth peace, good will toward men.

The End

Source: *A Dream Story: The Christmas Angel* by Henry Van Dyke (1852-1933), first published in his collection, *The Spirit of Christmas* (New York: C. Scribner's Sons, 1905).

A Pilgrimage To Bethlehem

Cast
Storyteller 1
Storyteller 2
Gregory
Ivan
Peasant Man
Peasant Woman
Gregory's Wife

(The Storytellers remain seated or standing throughout the per-formance, as the director chooses. The other actors sit until they make their "entrances," then they stand)

Storyteller 1: Once in Russia there lived two men who had decided to go on a pilgrimage to the Holy Land. One of them was a well-to-do farmer named Ivan Petroff, who was short and had curly hair.

Storyteller 2: The other, Gregory Radinsky, was not so well off. He was tall and quite bald. The two men had taken a vow years before to go to the holy places together. Gregory longed especially to go to Bethlehem to see the site of Jesus' birth.

Storyteller 1: Ivan, however, could never spare the time. He always had some important business at hand. As soon as he finished one thing, he started another.

Storyteller 2: One day the two men met outside of Ivan's house.

Gregory: Well, Ivan, when are we going to fulfill our vow?

Ivan: We must wait, Gregory. This year has turned out to be a hard one for me. I started to build this new house thinking that it would cost me something over 100 rubles, but now it's getting on to 200 and it's still not finished. We will have to wait until next year. Next year, God willing, we will go without fail.

Gregory: That's what you said last year. It seems to me that we ought not to put it off, but should go at once. This year is the best time.

Ivan: The time is right enough, but what about my house? How can I leave that?

Gregory: As if you had no one to leave in charge! Your son can look after it.

Ivan: But how? My son is not trustworthy; he sometimes takes a glass too much.

Gregory: Oh, neighbor, when we die they'll get on without us very well. Let your son begin now to get some experience.

Ivan: That's true enough, but somehow, when one begins a thing, one likes to see it done.

Gregory: Friend, we can never get through all we have to do. A few weeks ago, my family was washing and cleaning for Easter. Here something needed doing, there something else, and we couldn't get everything done. So my daughter-in-law, who's a very sensible girl, said "We may be thankful that the holiday comes without waiting for us, for however hard we worked, we should never be ready."

Ivan: I've spent a lot of money on this house and one can't start a journey with empty pockets. We will need 100 rubles apiece — and that's no small sum.

Gregory: Now, come, come, old friend. You have ten times as much as I, and yet you talk about money. Only say when we are to start, and though I have nothing now, I will have enough by then.

Ivan: *(Smiling)* Dear me, I did not know you were so rich! Why, where will you get it?

Gregory: I can scrape some together at home, and I'll sell some of my beehives to my neighbor. He's been wanting to buy them for a long time.

Ivan: If the bees swarm well this year, you'll regret it.

Gregory: Regret it! Not I, neighbor. I have never regretted anything in my life, except my sins. There's nothing more precious than the soul.

Ivan: That's so. Still, it's not right to neglect things at home.

Gregory: But what if our souls are neglected? That's worse. We took the vow, so let's go. I'm getter old and I don't want to die without seeing Bethlehem and the place was Jesus was born. Now, seriously, let us go.

(Pause)

Ivan: You are right. Let us go. Life and death are in the hands of God. We must go now while we are still healthy and have our strength.

Storyteller 2: A week later, the two men were ready.

Storyteller 1: Ivan had money enough on hand.

Storyteller 2: Gregory sold ten of his beehives to his neighbor for seventy rubles. The other thirty he scraped together from members of his family.

Storyteller 1: So the two men started out. Their families packed food for them.

Storyteller 2: They put on their new leather shoes.

Storyteller 1: And everyone went with them to the edge of the village and wished them well.

Storyteller 1: As they finally began their pilgrimage, Gregory was in a cheerful mood. Soon he had forgotten all of his affairs at home and began to sing.

(Ivan improvises a hymn)

Storyteller 2: Ivan, however, was weighted down with household cares.

Ivan: I wonder if I have forgotten to tell my son something important. I hope he remembers to plant the potatoes on time. Oh, I should have warned him more firmly about his drinking. And what if he sells the pigs too cheaply?

Storyteller 1: The two men walked for five weeks. At first, when people discovered that they were pilgrims headed for the Holy Land, they vied with one another in asking them into their homes. They took them in and fed them and would accept no payment and sometimes even put bread or cakes into their bags.

Storyteller 2: Eventually, however, they crossed into a district where the harvest had failed. The peasants gave them free lodging for the night, but no longer fed them for nothing. Sometimes they could get no bread; they offered to pay for it but there was none to be had.

Storyteller 1: As they were walking along one warm day, Gregory became hot, tired, and thirsty. Ivan was the better walker of the two and Gregory found it hard to keep up.

Gregory: If I could only have a drink of water.

Ivan: Well then, friend, have one. Myself, I don't need one.

Gregory: Then you go on, Ivan. I'll just go up to that little hut there and ask for some water. I will catch up with you in a moment.

Ivan: All right. Take your time and enjoy your drink.

Storyteller 2: Gregory entered the yard and saw a man lying on the ground.

Gregory: Hello, sir. May I have a drink of water?

Storyteller 1: But the man gave no answer. Gregory thought,

Gregory: Either he is sick or unfriendly.

Storyteller 2: Then Gregory heard a child crying. He decided to knock on the door of the hut.

(Storyteller 2 knocks on the side of his book, or on his/her stool or chair)

Gregory: Hello, masters!

Storyteller 1: No answer.

Gregory: Hello, Christians!

Storyteller 2: Nothing stirred.

Gregory: Hey, servants of God!

Storyteller 1: Still no reply.

Gregory: Dear me, some misfortune must have happened to these people. I had better take a look.

Storyteller 2: Gregory opened the door and entered the hut.

Storyteller 1: A woman sat on a bench. Near her was a thin, wax-colored boy with a protruding stomach, crying.

Storyteller 2: The air in the hut was foul. Gregory looked around and saw a girl lying near the oven with her eyes closed and her throat rattling.

Storyteller 1: The woman managed to lift her head and speak.

Woman: *(Weakly)* What do you want? ... What do you want, man? ... We have nothing, nothing.

Gregory: I came in for a drink of water, servant of God.

Woman: We have nothing to fetch it in ... go your way.

Gregory: Is there no one among you, then, well enough to attend to that girl?

Woman: No, we have no one. That is my daughter. My husband is dying outside and we are dying in here.

Storyteller 2: Gregory was about to question the woman again, when the man staggered into the hut. Clinging to the walls, he fell in the corner.

Man: *(Weakly)* Sickness has seized us ... and famine. My children are dying of hunger.

Storyteller 1: Opening his bag, Gregory took out a loaf of bread and, cutting off a piece with his knife, he handed it to the man. The man would not take it, but pointed to his children.

Man: Give it to them.

Storyteller 2: When the boy smelled the bread, he seized the slice and bit into it so that his nose disappeared in the chunk.

Storyteller 1: Then Gregory cut off another piece and gave it to the girl and she, too, began munching it.

Woman: If only you could bring some water. Their mouths are parched. I tried to fetch some water yesterday — or was it today — I can't remember, but I fell down and could go no further. The bucket remained there, unless some one has taken it.

Storyteller 2: Gregory went to the well, found the bucket, and brought some water for the people to drink. The man, the woman, and the two children ate some more bread with the water.

Storyteller 1: Presently, Gregory went to the village shop and bought some millet, flour, and oil.

Storyteller 2: He found the ax, chopped some wood, and built a fire. Then he boiled some soup and gave the starving people a meal.

Storyteller 1: When the family had regained some strength, the man and woman began telling Gregory how they had sunk to their present state.

Woman: We were poor enough before, but when the crops failed, what we harvested hardly lasted us through the autumn. We had nothing left by the time winter came, and had to beg from our neighbors and from anyone we could. At first they gave, but then they began to refuse. Some would have been glad enough to help us, but they had nothing to give, and we were ashamed of asking. We were in debt everywhere.

Man: I went to look for work, but could find none. Everywhere people were offering to work, merely for their own keep. One day you'd get a short job, and then you might spend two days looking for work again. My wife and daughter went begging further away. But they got very little; bread was so scarce. Still, we scraped food together somehow and hoped to struggle through until next harvest. And then, sickness seized us. Things became worse and worse. One day you might have something to eat, and then nothing for two days. We began eating grass. Finally, I had no strength left and couldn't keep on my feet and there was no one to help us recover.

Woman: I struggled on alone for a while, but at last I broke down for want of food and grew quite weak. My daughter also grew weak and timid. I told her to go to the neighbors, but she would not leave the hut and crept into a corner and sat there.

Man: The day before yesterday a neighbor looked in, but seeing that we were ill and hungry she turned away and left. Poor woman, she has nothing for her own little ones to eat.

Woman: And so we lay, waiting for death.

Storyteller 2: Having heard their story, Gregory gave up any thought of catching up to his comrade that day and remained with the family that night.

Storyteller 1: In the morning, he got up and began doing the housework, just as if it were his own home.

Storyteller 2: The family had sold everything to buy bread — cooking utensils, clothing, and all. So Gregory began replacing what was necessary, making some things and buying others. Finally, he thought,

Gregory: Well, I never expected to waste so much time on the way. I really must be getting on.

Storyteller 1: The next day, however, was the feast day of Saints Peter and Paul, and Gregory thought,

Gregory: I will stay and celebrate the day with these people. I will go and buy them something and keep the feast with them. The next day I will start out again.

Storyteller 2: So, Gregory went to the village and bought milk, wheat flour, and pork drippings and helped the woman bake for the next day.

Storyteller 1: On the feast day, Gregory and the family went to church and ate a good meal in the hut.

Storyteller 2: The man, meanwhile, went to the rich landlord to whom he had mortgaged his plow, land, and meadow to buy food. He begged the landlord to grant him use of the land until after the harvest, but the landlord refused. The poor man came back very sad and began to weep.

Gregory: How are they to live now? Other people will go hay-making, but there will be nothing for them to mow since their grass land is mortgaged. The rye will ripen. Others will reap (and what a fine crop mother earth is giving this year), but they have nothing to look forward to. Their three acres are pledged to an-other man. When I am gone, they'll drift back into the state I found them in.

Storyteller 1: That night, Gregory said his prayers and lay down to sleep.

Storyteller 2: But he could not sleep.

Storyteller 1: On the one hand,

Gregory: I have spent too much time and money as it was.

Storyteller 2: On the other hand,

Gregory: I feel sorry for these unfortunate people ... There seems to be no end to it. First, I only meant to bring them a little water and give each of them a slice of bread. Just see where it has landed me. Now, it's a case of redeeming the meadow and the cornfield. And when I have done that, I will have to buy a cow for them and a horse for the man to plow with. A nice fix you've gotten yourself into, Gregory. You'll never reach Bethlehem at this rate.

Storyteller 1: He thought and thought.

Gregory: I ought to be going.

Storyteller 2: Yet pity held him back.

Gregory: I don't know what to do.

Storyteller 1: Gregory woke in the morning and said to himself,

Gregory: Today, I will redeem their field and will buy them a horse and a cow. If I leave these people in need and go to seek the Lord in the Holy Land, I may actually lose him.

Storyteller 2: Gregory heard that there was a horse and cow for sale at the public house. He struck a bargain with the owner and bought them.

Storyteller 1: Very early the next morning, while everyone was asleep, Gregory got up, put on his shoes, packed his bag, and set off to follow Ivan.

Storyteller 2: When he had gotten a little way from the village, he stopped to count his money and was surprised to find that he had only seventeen rubles left.

Gregory: Well, it is no use trying to get to the Holy Land with this. It's not nearly enough. My friend Ivan will get to the Holy Land without me. I'm sure he will light a candle at the shrine in

Bethlehem in my name. As for me, I'm afraid I shall never fulfill my vow in this life. I must trust in an all-merciful God who will pardon me for not keeping the vow.

Storyteller 1: When Gregory reached home, his family was delighted to see him and asked many questions.

Storyteller 2: Why and how had he been left behind?

Storyteller 1: Why had he returned without reaching Bethlehem?

Storyteller 2: But Gregory only said,

Gregory: It was not God's will that I should get there. I lost my money on the way and lagged behind my companion. Forgive me, for God's sake.

Storyteller 1: Ivan's family heard of Gregory's return and came for news of him.

Gregory: Ivan is a fast walker. We parted three days before Peter and Paul Day. I meant to catch up with him, but all sorts of things happened. I lost my money and had no means to get any further. So I turned back.

Storyteller 2: The villagers were astonished that so sensible a man as Gregory should have acted so foolishly and lost his money. But they soon forgot all about it.

Storyteller 1: The day that Gregory had stopped at the hut of the starving people, Ivan had waited for him.

Storyteller 2: He waited and waited.

Storyteller 1: He took a nap, woke up, and again sat waiting.

Storyteller 2: His friend never came. So, Ivan thought,

Ivan: Perhaps, he has passed me. Or perhaps, someone gave him a ride and he drove by while I slept and did not see me ... But how could he not help seeing me? One can see so far out here on the steppes ... Should I go back? ... Suppose he is in front of me, then we will miss each other completely and it will be worse. I had better go on. We will be sure to meet up when we both stop for the night.

Storyteller 1: Ivan went on, asking everyone that he met whether they had seen a tall, bald man.

Storyteller 2: No one had seen such a traveler.

Storyteller 1: Ivan wondered about his friend, but went on alone, saying,

Ivan: We will be sure to meet in Odessa, or on board the ship.

Storyteller 2: But, Ivan did not find Gregory in Odessa or on board the ship.

Storyteller 1: Ivan finally arrived in the Holy Land and began visiting all the shrines.

Ivan: *(In awe and wonder)* Abraham's monastery and the place where Abraham intended to sacrifice his son! ... The spot where Christ appeared to Mary Magdalene! ... Bethany, the village of Mary, Martha, and Lazarus! ... The River Jordan, where John the Baptist baptized Jesus! ... The Church of the Holy Sepulcher, the spot where Jesus rose from the dead!

Storyteller 2: At every holy place he visited, Ivan attended services, lit candles, and said prayers for his loved ones.

Storyteller 1: He took water from the River Jordan and some earth from Nazareth.

Storyteller 2: But as awed as he was, Ivan was not above the occasional grumble.

Ivan: At every holy place you visit, there seems to be some monk with his hand out asking for money for the upkeep of the shrine. You'd think that the inns and hostels would give a discount to pilgrims.

Storyteller 1: During his third week there, he traveled to Bethlehem and attended mass at the Church of the Holy Nativity, the site of Jesus' birth. The church was so packed that he was forced to stand in the back.

Ivan: Oh, if only my friend Gregory could be here with me. He would be thrilled to finally see the spot where Jesus was born.

Storyteller 2: As he stood gazing at the oil lamps flickering above, he saw something that surprised him.

Storyteller 1: In the very front of the crowd, he saw a tall, bald-headed man with his arms outstretched praying ... who looked like Gregory.

Ivan: It looks like him, but it can't be Gregory. He could not have gotten ahead of me. The ship before ours started a week sooner and he could not have caught that one. He was not on our ship; I saw every pilgrim on board.

Storyteller 2: Hardly had Ivan thought this, when the tall man turned his head to the side and Ivan recognized him.

Ivan: That is Gregory Radinsky! That bald head, the eyes and nose, the expression on his face! I've known him all my life! I'd recognize him anywhere!

Storyteller 1: Ivan was very pleased that he had found his friend again and wondered how Gregory had gotten ahead of him.

Ivan: Well done, Gregory! Just see how he pushed ahead to the front. He must have come across someone who showed him how. Maybe he bribed someone. Perhaps he will show me how to get to the front, also.

Storyteller 2: When the service was over, the crowd began to push toward the tiny door to exit.

Ivan: Well, this time he will not escape me! I will go out and stand at the door. The door is so small that we can't miss each other.

Storyteller 1: Ivan went out and stood by the door while everyone passed out.

Storyteller 2: But Gregory did not appear.

Storyteller 1: Ivan searched the church and asked everyone,

Ivan: Have you seen a tall, bald-headed Russian pilgrim?

Storyteller 2: But Gregory was no where to be found.

Storyteller 1: Ivan finally gave up looking for his friend. He stayed in the Holy Land for another few days and then started homeward.

Storyteller 2: He traveled the same road he had come by. When he came to the district where he had parted with Gregory, he thought,

Ivan: I may as well ask about Gregory. I think this is the very hut he went to for a drink of water.

Storyteller 1: The woman of the house greeted him warmly.

Woman: Come in, come in, Sir. Have supper and spend the night with us.

Storyteller 2: She brought him water to wash himself, made him sit down at the table, then set milk, curd cakes, and porridge before him.

Woman: We have good reason to welcome pilgrims. It was a pilgrim who showed us what life is. We reached such a pass this summer, that we lay ill and helpless with nothing to eat. We should have died, but God sent us a man to help us — just such as you. He came in one day to ask for a drink of water, saw the state we were in, took pity on us, and stayed with us. He gave us food and drink and set us on our feet again. He redeemed our land and bought us a horse and a cow.

Man: We don't know whether he was a man or an angel from God. He loved us, pitied us, and went away without even telling us his name, so that we don't even know whom to pray for. I can see it all before me now. There I lay, waiting for death, when in comes a tall, bald man. He was not much to look at and he asked for a drink of water. I, a sinner, thought to myself: "What does he come prowling around here for?" And just think what he did! As soon as he saw us, he put down his bag, opened it, and gave us bread.

Woman: Had he not come, we should have died in our sins. We were dying in despair, murmuring against God and man. But he set us on our feet again. And through him, we learned to know God and to believe that there is good in man. May the Lord bless him!

Storyteller 1: That night, Ivan could not sleep. He could not get Gregory out of his mind, but remembered how he had seen him in Bethlehem standing in the foremost place.

Ivan: So that is how he got ahead of me ... God may or may not have accepted my pilgrimage, but he has certainly accepted Gregory's.

Storyteller 2: The next morning Ivan bid farewell to the family and continued his journey.

Storyteller 1: When he got home, he had a warm reunion with his family.

Storyteller 2: Though he wasn't all that pleased with the job his son had done in his absence.

Storyteller 1: Early the next day, he went to see his friend Gregory. He was met in the front yard by Gregory's wife.

Gregory's Wife: How do you do, neighbor? How do you do, good friend? Did you get to the Holy Land safely?

Ivan: Yes, thank God. I have been there and back. I lost sight of your husband, but I hear he got home safely.

Gregory's Wife: Yes, neighbor, he has come back. He's been back a long time. Just before Dormition Day, I think it was, he returned. We were glad the Lord sent him back to us. It was dull here without him. It's more cheerful when he's at home. And how glad our son was. He said, "It's like being without sunlight when Papa's away." It was dull without him, dear friend. We love him and take good care of him.

Ivan: Is he home now?

Gregory's Wife: He is. He is with his bees. He says that they are swarming well this year. The Lord has given such strength to the bees, that my husband doesn't remember the like. "The Lord is not rewarding us according to our sins," he says. Come in; he will be glad to see you.

Storyteller 2: Ivan passed through the yard to the back and there was Gregory, standing under the birch trees, looking upward, his arms outstretched and his bald head shining, just as Ivan had seen him in Bethlehem.

38

Storyteller 1: The golden bees flew around his head like a halo.

Gregory's Wife: Here is your friend come to visit.

Storyteller 2: Gregory looked around with a pleased face, gently picking bees out of his beard.

Gregory: Good day, neighbor. Welcome back, old friend. Did you get to the Holy Land safely?

Ivan: My feet walked there. And I brought you some water from the River Jordan. Whether the Lord accepted my efforts, I don't know.

Gregory: Well, the Lord be thanked! May Christ bless us!

(Pause)

Ivan: My feet have been to the Holy Land, but whether my soul or another's has been there more truly ...

Gregory: That's God's business, neighbor. God's business.

Ivan: On my return journey, I stopped at the hut where you remained behind.

Storyteller 1: Gregory became alarmed and said hurriedly,

Gregory: God's business, neighbor. God's business. Come into the house. I'll give you some of our honey.

Storyteller 2: Gregory changed the conversation and talked of home affairs.

Storyteller 1: Ivan never spoke to Gregory about the people in the hut or how he had seen him in Bethlehem.

Storyteller 2: He now understood that the best way to keep one's vows to God and to do his will is for each one, while he lives, to show love and do good to others.

Storyteller 1: Ivan was never sure which one of them had truly been to Bethlehem.

The End

Source: The short story, "Two Old Men," written by Leo Tolstoy (1828-1910) in 1885. The story first appeared in English in *Thirty-three Tales*, translated by Aylmer and Louise Maude (London and New York: H. Frowde, 1906).

Two Babes In The Manger

Cast
Storyteller 1
Storyteller 2
Teacher
Misha

(Storytellers 1 and 2 stand at left and right. The Teacher stands in the center. Misha remains seated until he "enters." An adult can play the part of Misha, but the piece is more effective if a child takes the role)

Storyteller 1: Soon after the fall of the Soviet Union, the Russian Department of Education invited two American Christian teachers to give a series of courses on biblical principles in Russian public institutions.

Storyteller 2: The two Americans taught in prisons, to police and fire departments, and at military installations. One of their stops was a large orphanage for children who had been abused or abandoned.

Storyteller 1: Since it was nearing the Christmas season, one of the teachers decided to tell the children, through the Russian translator, the story of the birth of Jesus.

Teacher: Mary and Joseph arrived in Bethlehem but, because of all the travelers, they could not find a room in any of the inns. The couple went to the stable, with all the animals, and there Jesus was born. Since they had no cradle for him, they laid Jesus in a manger. In the fields nearby, there were shepherds ...

Storyteller 2: Throughout the story the children listened in amazement. They had never heard this story before.

Storyteller 1: When she had finished the story, the teacher opened up a box she had brought with her.

Teacher: Boys and girls, I have brought with me, from America, a box of colored paper and cardboard and strips of felt. I'm going to give each of you a few pieces and I will teach you how to make a Nativity scene of your own — with Mary, Joseph, the manger, and the baby Jesus.

Storyteller 1: The children, who had never had much in the way of play things or art supplies, were delighted. They busily set about cutting, tearing, and folding the materials.

Storyteller 2: The teacher walked around the room examining what the children were doing. She was very pleased.

Teacher: My, they certainly have come up with an amazing variety of Nativity scenes.

(Misha stands)

Storyteller 1: Finally, she came to little Misha, a boy of about six, and was startled to find that he had ... *two* babies in his manger.

Teacher: Oh, dear! No, no, Misha!

Storyteller 2: So she said to the translator,

Teacher: Tell him there is only one baby in the manger.

Storyteller: But, through the translator, little Misha insisted,

Misha: No, no. Two babies!

Teacher: He must have misunderstood me. Ask him why he has two babies in his manger.

Storyteller 1: The little boy responded, through the translator, by retelling the story that he had just heard.

Misha: An angel appeared to a young woman named Mary and told her that she would be the mother of the Savior of the world ...

Storyteller 2: Misha recounted the story with great accuracy ... until he came to the part where Mary put Jesus in the manger. Then it became his story.

Misha: And when Mary laid the baby in the manger, little Jesus looked at me and asked me if I had a place to stay. I told him that I had no mama and no papa, so I didn't have a place to stay. Then, Jesus told me that I could stay with him. I told him that I didn't have a gift for him, like everybody else. Jesus said that I could keep him warm and that would be the best gift anybody ever gave him. I got into the manger with him and Jesus looked at me and told me that I could stay with him — for always.

Storyteller 1: The teachers, the translator, and the orphanage staff all had tears in their eyes. Little Misha had understood the story of the birth of Jesus better than any of them.

Storyteller 2: For the birth of Jesus means that, no matter who or what we are, there is always a place for us in the manger and that we can stay with Jesus — for always.

The End

Source: An anonymous story that appeared on several sites on the internet. It is presumed to be true.

The Tree That Didn't Get Trimmed

We know that in everything God works for good with those who love him, who are called according to his purpose. — Romans 8:28

O the depth of the riches and wisdom and knowledge of God! How unsearchable are his judgments and how inscrutable his ways! For who has known the mind of the Lord, or who has been his counselor?
— Romans 11:33-34

Cast
Storyteller 1
Storyteller 2
Fir Tree
Actor 1 (plays Woodsman and Grocer)
Actor 2 (plays Lady Shopper and Farmer's Wife)
Actor 3 (plays Child, Customer 1, and Cemetery Man)
Actor 4 (plays Customer 2 and Farmer)

(The two Storytellers stand at opposite ends of the playing area; the Tree stands in the center. Actors 1-4 sit slightly back until they "enter")

Storyteller 1: If you walk through a grove of balsam trees you will notice that the young trees are silent. They are listening.

Storyteller 2: But the old tall ones, especially the fir trees, are whispering.

Storyteller 1: They are telling the story of the tree that didn't get trimmed.

45

Storyteller 2: It sounds like a painful story, and the murmur of the old trees as they tell it is rather solemn, but it is an encouraging story for young saplings to hear.

Storyteller 1: On warm, autumn days when your trunk is tickled with ants and insects climbing, and the whole glade smells sweet, drowsy, and sad, and the hardwood trees are boasting of the gay colors they are beginning to show, many a young evergreen has been cheered by it.

Storyteller 2: The tree in this story should never have been cut down. He wouldn't have been, but it was getting dark in the Vermont woods and the woodsman with the ax said to himself,

Woodsman: Just one more.

Storyteller 1: He was a fine, well-grown young tree, but too tall for his age. His branches were

Woodsman: *(Disappointedly)* rather scraggly.

Storyteller 2: If he'd been left there, he would have been an unusually big tree some day. But now, he was at that awkward age and didn't have

Woodsman: the tapering shape and the thick, even foliage that people like on Christmas trees.

Storyteller 1: Worse still, instead of running up to a straight, clean spire, his top was

Woodsman: *(Disparagingly)* a bit lopsided, with a fork in it.

Storyteller 2: But the tree didn't know this as he stood with many others, leaning against the side wall of the grocer's shop. In those cold December days he was very happy, thinking

Tree: of the pleasure to come!

Storyteller 1: He had heard of

Tree: the delights of Christmas Eve! The setting up of the tree, the tinsel balls and colored toys and stars, the peppermint canes, and the ornaments of spun-glass!

Storyteller 2: Even that old anxiety of Christmas trees — burning candles — did not worry him, for he had been told that

Tree: nowadays people have strings of tiny electric lights that cannot set one on fire.

Storyteller 1: He looked forward to the great festival with a confident heart.

Tree: Oh, I shall be very grand. I hope there will be children to admire me. It must be a great moment when the children hang their stockings on you!

Storyteller 2: He even felt sorry for the first trees that were chosen and taken away.

Tree: It would be best not to be bought until Christmas Eve. Then, in the shining darkness, someone will pick me out, and away we will go. The tire chains will clank and jingle merrily on the snowy road.

Storyteller 1: He imagined a big house

Tree: with a fire glowing on the hearth, the hushed rustle of wrapping paper and parcels being unpacked. Someone will say

Child: Oh, what a beautiful tree!

Tree: How erect and stiff I will brace myself in my iron tripod stand!

Storyteller 2: But, day after day went by.

Storyteller 1: One by one, the other trees were taken.

Storyteller 2: He began to grow troubled.

Storyteller 1: For every customer who looked at him seemed to have an unkind word.

Customer 1: Too tall.

Customer 2: No, this one won't do. The branches are too skimpy.

Storyteller 2: So the grocer said,

Grocer: If I chop off the top, it wouldn't be so bad.

Storyteller 1: The tree shuddered, the customers passed on to look at others. Some of his branches ached

Tree: *(Sadly)* where the grocer bent them down to make my shape more attractive.

Storyteller 2: Across the street was a five-and-dime store. Its bright windows were full of scarlet odds and ends. When the door opened, he could see

Tree: people crowded along the aisles, cheerfully jostling one another with bumpy packages, flashes of marvelous color ... and ornaments for luckier trees.

Storyteller 1: He could hear

Tree: the buzz of talk, the shuffle of feet, the constant ringing of cash drawers.

Storyteller 2: Every evening, as Christmas drew nearer, the sidewalks were more crowded.

Storyteller 1: The handsomer trees, not as tall as he, but more bushy and shapely, were ranked in front of him.

Storyteller 2: Finally, he was shown to a lady who wanted

Woman Shopper: a tree very cheap.

Grocer: You can have this one for a dollar,

Storyteller 1: said the grocer. This was only a fourth of what the grocer had asked for him at first. Even so the lady refused.

Woman Shopper: No, no. I think I'll go across the street to the five-and-dime store and buy one of those nice artificial trees.

Storyteller 2: The grocer pushed him back carelessly and he toppled over on his side.

(Pause)

Storyteller 1: It was Christmas Eve. It was a foggy evening, with drizzling rain. The alley alongside the store was thick with trampled slush.

Storyteller 2: As he lay among the broken boxes and fallen scraps of holly, thoughts came to him. He remembered

Tree: the wintry sparkle of the woods, the big trees with crusts and clumps of silver snow on their broad boughs, the keen singing of the lonely wind.

Storyteller 2: He remembered

Tree: the strong, warm feeling of my roots reaching down into the safe earth. That is a good feeling. It means to a tree just what it means to humans to stretch their toes down toward the bottom of a well-tucked bed.

Storyteller 1: He had given up all that to lie here

Tree: *(Sadly)* disdained and forgotten, in a littered alley, with the splashing of feet and cars. No toys or stockings for me.

Storyteller 2: He trembled a bit with self-pity and shed some of his needles.

Storyteller 1: Late that night, after all the shopping was over, the grocer came to clear away what was left.

Storyteller 2: The boxes,

Storyteller 1: the broken wreaths,

Storyteller 2: the empty barrels,

Storyteller 1: and our tree, with one or two others that hadn't been sold, all were thrown through the side door into the cellar. As the unwanted trees lay on the stone floor of the dark cellar and watched the furnace flicker, our tree thought to himself,

Tree: So this is Christmas.

Storyteller 2: The day after Christmas a man came in who wanted some green boughs

Cemetery Man: to decorate the cemetery.

Storyteller 1: The grocer took the hatchet and seized the trees without ceremony. Our tree was

Tree: too disheartened to care.

Grocer: Chop, chop, chop,

Storyteller 2: went the blade and the sweet smelling branches were carried away. The naked trees were thrown in the corner.

Storyteller 1: And now our tree, what was left of him, had plenty of time to think.

Tree: How silly it was of me to imagine such a fine, happy career for myself. I feel sorry for the other young trees, still growing in the fresh hill country, who are dreaming the same unattainable dreams.

Storyteller 2: Now, perhaps you don't know what happens to left-over Christmas trees.

Storyteller 1: You could never guess.

Storyteller 2: Farmers come in from the country

Farmer: and buy them at five cents each to use as bean poles and grape arbors.

Storyteller 1: Perhaps —

Storyteller 2: here begins the encouraging part of the story —

Storyteller 1: Perhaps the trees are really happier, in the end, than the trees that get trimmed for Christmas.

Farmer: They go back into the fresh, moist earth of spring, and when the sun grows hot the quick tendrils of the vines climb up them and they are covered with beans or grapes.

Storyteller 2: One day the naked fir poles were thrown into the truck with many others and made

Tree: a rattling, bumpy journey out into the country.

Storyteller 1: The farmer unloaded them in his yard and was stacking them up by the barn, when his wife came out to watch him.

Farmer's Wife: There! That's just what I need, a nice, long pole with a fork in it. Jim, put that one over there to hold up my clothesline.

Farmer: Just as you say, dear.

Storyteller 2: It was the first time that anyone had praised our tree and his dried up heart swelled

Tree: with a tingle of forgotten sap.

Storyteller 1: They put him near one end of the clothesline, with his stump close to the flower bed. The fork that had been despised for a Christmas star was

Farmer's Wife: just the thing to hold up a clothesline.

Storyteller 2: It was wash day, and soon the farmer's wife began bringing out wet garments

Farmer's Wife: to dry and freshen in the clean, bright air.

Storyteller 1: The very first thing that hung near the top of the Christmas pole was

Tree: a cluster of children's stockings!

Storyteller 2: That isn't quite the end of the story, as the old fir trees whisper it in the breeze.

Storyteller 1: The tree that didn't get trimmed was so cheerful —

Tree: watching the stockings and other colorful clothes that plumbed out in the wind just as though waiting to be spanked —

Storyteller 1: that he didn't notice what was going on, or up, below him.

Storyteller 2: A vine had caught hold of his trunk and was steadily twisting upward.

Storyteller 1: One morning, when the farmer's wife came out, intending to shift him, she stopped and exclaimed.

Farmer's Wife: Why, I mustn't move this pole. The morning glory has run right up it.

Storyteller 2: And so it had. Our bare pole was blue and crimson with the color of morning glories ... as pretty as any Christmas tree.

Storyteller 1: Something nice, the old firs believe, always happens to the trees that don't get trimmed.

The End

Source: *The Tree That Didn't Get Trimmed* by Christopher Morley (1890-1957), which was printed in the December, 1925 issue of *Country Life* magazine.

Willibald Krautman's Trip To Heaven

Cast
Storyteller
Willibald Krautman
Saint Peter
Wife

(Storyteller sits or stands off to one side. Willibald stands at center. Wife sits facing away from the audience until she "enters." Saint Peter sits until his "entrance," when he stands on his chair)

Storyteller: Willibald Krautman and Christmas — these two things belonged together like a door and its hinges, like a clock and its face, like a bell and its tower. The whole year long, Willibald Krautman thought about, dreamt about, and prepared things for Christmas. During his life, Willibald had carved more than 1,000 Nativity figures, he had built more than sixty manger scenes, and he had attended every cribmakers' conference in Innsbruck in the Austrian Tyrol. Often his soul would inflate itself and whisper into his ear,

Willibald: Willibald, after all, you are the greatest artist and Nativity carver throughout the whole land. There is no one who can be compared to you. There will hardly be a single soul who will be so highly respected in heaven as you. Surely when you die and go to heaven some day, they will fling open the golden gates and lead you in triumph.

Storyteller: It just so happened that God called Willibald Krautman, and right on Christmas Eve. As he was trotting up the steep road to heaven, he began talking to himself, as he frequently did.

Willibald: Do you see, my dear Willibald, how the Christ Child honors those who honor him? He is having you called to heaven just on Christmas Eve, the most beautiful feast day in heaven! Perhaps they are calling you up there just so you can repair the heavenly crib scene. Well, well!

Storyteller: His thoughts about the heavenly Christmas manger scene seemed to slow him down. The road was long, and it was wintertime and cold. The path seemed to get narrower and steeper. A few times, he slid on the icy path and slid back a few steps. This annoyed him, and he began to grumble to himself.

Willibald: If they really want me, they could at least have sent a carriage for me. That certainly isn't asking too much. And what are all those angels in heaven doing? Not a single one is here to meet me and help me! After all, I'm not an ordinary traveler; they should know that!

Storyteller: But despite all his grumbling and muttering, *(Willibald makes indistinguishable muttering and grumbling noises)* no band of angels appeared and no heavenly carriage arrived. Willibald trudged wearily onward. It grew colder and darker. He was so exhausted he sat down on a rock to rest. Finally he saw it — in the distance — the heavenly Jerusalem. It stood on a high mountain of bright silver, and the walls and buildings were made of the purest gold. Inside the city, a bright light was shining, 1,000 times brighter than the sun, but milder and softer. Though worn out, Willibald rushed to the gates of pearl and gold and knocked. *(Willibald knocks on the side of his book)* Nobody came. He knocked again. *(Willibald knocks again on the side of his book)* Still nobody came.

Willibald: Well, isn't anyone coming? Perhaps they aren't finished with their preparations for my welcome. Or maybe they think I'm still far off and have no idea I'm here already.

Storyteller: Finally, in exasperation, he stood on a star, waved his hand and shouted,

Willibald: Hello! Hello! Is anybody there? It's me, Willibald Krautman!

Storyteller: A little angel in a white robe stuck her head out of a window, looked around, and quickly disappeared.

Willibald: Well, now it's going to begin. The little angel is certainly going to announce me. All the bells will start to ring, cannons will be shot off, and choirs will begin to sing. Oh, how exciting!

Storyteller: But a half-hour went by and nobody came, nothing moved. There were no bells, no cannons, and no singing.

Willibald: Hmm, perhaps there are some rascally little angels playing a joke on me. I've carved enough angels in my time to know what fun they can be. I hope Saint Peter doesn't scold them too much.

Storyteller: Willibald finally decided to try to open the great doors himself. He pulled, and then he pushed, and then he rattled the portals. *(Willibald makes appropriate sound effects)*

Willibald: Hey, you little angels. Enough of this joke.

Storyteller: But the great doors didn't budge. Willibald, never a patient man on earth, was now getting impatient in heaven. He tried to get someone's attention. *(Willibald coughs several times)* Then he saw something he had never noticed before, a bell pull.

Willibald: Why, of course, I'm supposed to ring the bell.

Storyteller: And so he pulled and pulled and rang and rang. *(Willibald makes ringing sounds — "gdong, gding, gdong, gding," and so forth)* Finally, none other than Saint Peter himself, stuck his head out of a window.

Saint Peter: *(Standing on a chair)* Who's that pulling our gate bell out of its post? What kind of ruffian is down there, anyway?

Willibald: *(Proudly)* It is I, Willibald Krautman, well-known artist, carver of Nativity figures.

Saint Peter: Willibald Krautman! What an odd name! But you are not known to us. You must have taken a wrong turn. Did you expect to get in here?

Willibald: Well, of course. I've been waiting here for over an hour.

Saint Peter: Hmm, that is not a matter of course at all. Let me see if you are in the book.

Storyteller: Saint Peter disappeared *(Saint Peter gets down from the chair)* and left Willibald standing there with his mouth wide open. *(Willibald opens his mouth accordingly)*

Willibald: Well, thanks a lot for the friendly welcome! They don't know me in heaven; me, Willibald Krautman. They have to see if my name is in a book! The world can be ungrateful, but I would have thought that things would be different in heaven.

Storyteller: Suddenly, one of the great gates opens slightly and Saint Peter stepped out carrying a large book. He took a long time looking through the book. *(Saint Peter scans down his script with his finger as if looking for Willibald's name)*

Saint Peter: Kaufman, Kessler, Kissel. Yes, yes. Here you are, Willibald Krautman. *(Willibald smiles proudly, but Saint Peter frowns)* Willibald Krautman. But you cannot enter.

Willibald: I cannot enter! I'd like to ask the reason, if you please.

Saint Peter: Just listen. *(Reads from "the book")* You have been arrogant, vain, and overly proud of your work. You have considered others worthless in comparison to yourself and thought that nobody else could possibly make such beautiful Nativity figures.

Willibald: Well, it seems to me that you are making a great fuss over very little. You used to be a fisherman on earth, and a catcher of fish just has no idea what it is like to be an artist or how an artist feels. You don't say anything about the good things I have done. In my lifetime, I set up more than 100 Christmas crèches. My figures have awakened many thoughts of heaven in the human heart and have given many people much Christmas joy.

Saint Peter: Yes, that is true. But I can't just scratch out your arrogance.

Willibald: Every human being has some fault. I'm not so conceited as to think that I am one of the greatest saints. But one shouldn't make a big to-do over petty trifles.

Saint Peter: My good fellow, there are still some other things written down here. *(Proceeds to read from "the book")* You were lacking in patience. When a carving wasn't going smoothly under your hands, you broke out in anger.

Willibald: That was righteous anger. The devil could not stand my good work and often hid my tools or pushed over a stable so that all the figures rolled off onto the floor. Then, of course, a certain justifiable anger came over me.

Saint Peter: But, the things you said at those times were anything but quick prayers.

Willibald: Oh, for goodness sake. Who thinks about what he says in anger. That's not the sort of thing you should put on the golden scales. I have never done any real damage in anger *(Pauses)*, like other people. *(Pauses)* I never cut off anybody's ear.

Saint Peter: *(Coughs in embarrassment)* Well, now. If you want to make a court case out of this, you ought to have an advocate or a defender.

Willibald: Fine. Just let me come into heaven and I will find one.

Saint Peter: No, nothing impure can enter. You'll have to look down on earth for someone to speak for you.

Willibald: *(Sheepishly)* On earth? Well, I, that is, I unfortunately have no real friends on earth. I never had time for other people.

Saint Peter: Yes, there you have it. That's just what you don't have. Now I'm going to read the heaviest debt you have on your account. *(Reads from "book")* You have had far too little love for your neighbor. You have neglected to gain one friend or defender for yourself through a work of mercy.

Willibald: Well, I had to use all my money for the Christmas work I did.

Saint Peter: No Christmas expenses mean so much as a warm-hearted gift of love to people in need.

Willibald: But I always did a little bit.

Saint Peter: Yes, a little bit, but it was too little. Last year, for example, on Christmas Eve, you turned away a widow with three hungry children from your door.

Willibald: Last year I had to make a new design for the three kings and new figures for the flight to Egypt. And the kings needed to be gold-leafed. Those things cost money. My wood and art supplies were terribly expensive.

Saint Peter: Just the same, after you bought your wood and paint, you still had enough money left over to go to the tavern on Christmas

Eve — for a few drinks that were more than just to quench your thirst.

Willibald: Gracious, that was just a little joyful celebration because it was Christmas. The cheap wines that one gets nowadays are so bad that you only have to drink one glass and, snap *(Snaps his finger)* it goes right to your head.

Saint Peter: Now you're adding lying to your debts. Those were two bottles of the most expensive wine. You won't get far up here by lying. Lying is something that I just can't stand.

Willibald: Little white lies like that often come over the best people. *(Pauses)* Why, I read once about a man who lied his way out of bad situation *(Pauses)* three times before the cock crowed.

Saint Peter: *(Embarrassed)* Yes, but he wept about it the whole of the rest of his life. You try to cover up and soften your sins. *(Impatiently)* That's the end of my patience. Now, go where you belong.

Storyteller: Saint Peter, saying this, went back into heaven and slammed the door shut. *(Saint Peter slams his book shut.)* At last, Willibald realized fully the gravity of his situation. He knocked quite humbly and begged to be allowed in.

Willibald: *(Knocking softly on the side of his book)* Please, please let me in. I beg you.

Storyteller: But no one answered. He pulled on the bell rope, but it didn't make a sound. Inside everything was still. He almost crept around the side of the wall until he found a small crack. He peeked inside. Inside, he saw light and more and more light that he knew right away was the unending love that delights the heart and soul. Then he heard what seemed like a million voices singing, "Gloria in excelsis Deo. Glory to God in the highest and on earth peace to men of good will." Then an enormous longing came over him, a pain so great that he felt like he would die all over again. He wanted to scream, but he could not. All he could do was to whimper from the bottom of his heart,

Willibald: Forgive me my sins. Dear God, forgive me my sins. I am a sinner. Forgive me, I beg you.

Storyteller: He began to weep, softly at first, then louder. He pressed his head against the wall, sobbing. Suddenly there was a crack. *(Stamps his/her foot)* Then he felt something pulling and tearing at his feet. He plunged down and down and down. *(Willibald groans loudly)* He heard a well-known voice,

Wife: What's the matter? What's wrong, for heaven's sake?

Storyteller: He opened his eyes. He was in his own warm bed, in his own room. Beside him stood his wife, shaking him by the shoulder. It was clear to him that he was being awakened from a deep dream.

Wife: What's the matter with you, you silly fool? You were moaning and groaning as if somebody had cut off your ear.

Willibald: I have been in heaven.

Wife: A funny kind of heaven where you yell and scream like that.

Willibald: You don't understand. I will tell you all about it sometime.

Storyteller: But Willibald Krautman only told his wife half of what he experienced. He did become more and more thoughtful, and during every Christmas season, he lost a large sum of money — at least his wife believed he had lost it. Willibald became friendly and kind to everyone and no longer spoke impatiently. This year, he finally told his best friend — yes, he now had one — the whole story of his trip to heaven.

The End

Source: *Krippenmachers Himmelgang* by Reimmichl, the pen name of Father Sebastian Rieger (1867-1953). The story is from his collection, *Weihnacht in Tirol* (published by Verlagsanstalt Tyrolia, Innsbruck, Austria in 1911). Translated with the aid of computer software.

Two Christmas Dinners

*... every man shall give as he is able, according to the
blessing of the Lord your God which he has given you.*
— Deuteronomy 16:17

*Give to him who begs from you, and do not refuse him
who would borrow from you.* — Matthew 5:42

*In all things I have shown you that by so toiling one
must help the weak, remembering the words of the Lord
Jesus, how he said, "It is more blessed to give than to
receive."* — Acts 20:35

*And he said, "Truly, I tell you, this poor widow has put
in more than all of you; for all have contributed out of
their abundance, but she out of her poverty put in all
the living that she had."* — Luke 21:3-4

In this play, based on an O. Henry short story, the receiver
gives and the giver receives.

Cast
Storyteller 1
Storyteller 2
Snuffy Pete
Mr. Cabot
Waitress
Nurse (Waitress and Nurse could be played by the same actor)

*(The Storytellers are seated at stage left and stage right. In the
center of the stage are two small benches. Mr. Cabot, Waitress,
and Nurse sit upstage, facing away from the audience until they
"enter." Snuffy Pete is seated on the right bench, with stomach
extended, looking stuffed and uncomfortable)*

65

Storyteller 1: Snuffy Pete took his seat on the second bench as you enter Union Station from the east. Every Christmas Day, for nine years, he had taken his seat there promptly at one o'clock. Every time he had done so, things had happened to him —

Snuffy: Charles Dickensy things —

Storyteller 1: Things that swelled his waistcoat above his heart.

Storyteller 2: But today, Snuffy Pete's appearance at the annual meeting place seemed to have been the result of habit, rather than of hunger, which,

Snuffy: "charitable people" seem to think, afflicts the poor only during the holidays.

Storyteller 1: Certainly Pete was not hungry.

Storyteller 2: He had just come from a feast that had robbed him of his powers, barely leaving those of respiration and locomotion.

Storyteller 1: His breath came in short wheezes.

Storyteller 2: Buttons that had been sewn on his clothes by kind Salvation Army fingers, a week before, flew off like popcorn.

Storyteller 1: For Snuffy Pete was overcharged with the calories produced by a super bountiful dinner.

Snuffy: *(Licking his lips and rubbing his stomach)* Beginning with oysters and ending with plum pudding, and, in between, all the roast turkey with gravy and cornbread dressing and baked potatoes and candied yams and chicken salad and squash pie and ice cream in the world.

Storyteller 2: Therefore, he sat, gorged, and gazed upon the world with after-dinner contentment.

Snuffy: The meal was an unexpected one.

Storyteller 1: Pete was passing a red brick mansion on Fifth Avenue, in which lived two elderly ladies of ancient family and a reverence for traditions.

Snuffy: One of their traditions, it seems, was to station a servant at the gate with orders to admit the first hungry wayfarer who came along after the hour of noon ... and banquet him to a finish.

Storyteller 2: Snuffy Pete happened to pass on his way to the park, and the kind ladies gathered him in and upheld the custom of the house.

(Pause)

Storyteller 1: Suddenly, Pete's eyes bulged out fearfully. For Mr. Cabot, the old gentleman, was coming across Fourth Avenue toward his bench.

(Mr. Cabot stands and faces the audience)

Storyteller 2: Every Christmas Day, for nine years, Mr. Cabot had come there and found Snuffy Pete on his bench.

Snuffy: That is a thing that the old gentleman is trying to make a tradition.

Storyteller 1: Every Christmas Day, for nine years, Mr. Cabot found Snuffy there and led him to a restaurant and watched him eat a big dinner.

Storyteller 2: The old gentleman moved, straight and stately, toward the tradition that he was building.

(Mr. Cabot crosses to Snuffy's bench)

Snuffy: I don't think I can eat another morsel.

Storyteller 1: As his established benefactor came up, Snuffy Pete wheezed and shuddered. He would have run away, but nothing could separate him from his bench. Well had the two ladies done their work.

Mr. Cabot: Good morning. I am glad to perceive that the vicissitudes of another year have spared you to move in health about this beautiful world. For that blessing alone, this Christmas Day is well proclaimed to each of us. If you will come with me, my good man, I will provide you with a dinner that should make your physical being accord with the mental.

Storyteller 2: The old gentleman, apparently, had no relatives of his own. He lived alone in rented rooms in one of the old brownstone buildings.

Storyteller 1: He had adopted Pete as his Christmas family and tradition.

Snuffy: *(To Mr. Cabot)* Oh, you really shouldn't, Mr. Cabot.

Mr. Cabot: I insist. Isn't that what Christmas is all about, giving to our fellow man?

Snuffy: *(To audience)* The old gentleman's eyes are always bright with the pleasure of giving. How can I say no to him?

Storyteller 2: Snuffy Pete made a noise that sounded like peas bubbling in a pot. Speech was intended, and the old gentleman construed it as Snuffy's acceptance.

Snuffy: *(Weakly and not meaning a word of what he's saying)* Thank you kindly, sir. I'll go with you and much obliged ... I'm ... very hungry.

Storyteller 1: His near-coma had not prevented it from entering into Snuffy Pete's head that he was now a tradition.

Snuffy: My Christmas appetite is not my own.

Storyteller 2: It belonged to all the sacred rights of established custom. Snuffy Pete knew that he was the only one to whom the old gentleman could give every Christmas.

Storyteller 1: Mr. Cabot led his annual protégé southward toward the restaurant and to the table where the feast always occurred.

(Snuffy and Mr. Cabot cross to the bench at left and sit)

Storyteller 2: They were recognized and the waitress commented,

Waitress: Here comes the old guy who treats that same bum to a meal every Christmas.

Storyteller 1: Mr. Cabot sat across from the table glowing like a pearl. The waitress heaped the table with holiday food.

Storyteller 2: Snuffy Pete, with a sigh that was mistaken for hunger's expression, raised knife and fork and carved for himself a crown of imperishable laurel.

Mr. Cabot: *(With a big smile)* Don't be bashful, Mr. Pete. Dig in and eat heartily!

Storyteller 1: No more valiant hero ever fought his way through the ranks of the enemy.

Snuffy: *(Holding his stomach and looking pained, as if he might be sick at any moment)* Soup ... salad ... turkey ... pork chops ... mashed potatoes ... vegetables ... two kinds of pie!

Storyteller 2: Gorged nearly to bursting when he entered the restaurant, the smell of food had almost caused him to lose his honor as a gentleman, but he rallied like a true knight.

Storyteller 1: He saw the look of beneficent happiness on the old gentleman's face and he did not have the heart to see it fade.

Snuffy: *(Clutching his stomach)* The old gentleman seems to enjoy this so much. *(Snuffy obviously is not)*

Storyteller 2: In an hour, Snuffy leaned back with the battle won.

Snuffy: *(Barely able to talk)* Thank you kindly, sir. Thank you very much for a ... delicious meal.

Mr. Cabot: *(Still smiling)* You're very welcome, Mr. Pete. I assure you it was my pleasure to see you eat so heartily. It has made my Christmas merry, indeed.

Storyteller 1: Then, Snuffy Pete rose heavily with glazed eyes.

(Snuffy and Mr. Cabot stand up)

Storyteller 2: Mr. Cabot carefully counted out $1.30 in change, leaving three nickels for the waitress.

Storyteller 1: They parted as they did every year at the door, Mr. Cabot going south, Snuffy north.

(Snuffy crosses to the bench at right)

Storyteller 2: Around the corner Snuffy turned and stood for a minute. Then he seemed to puff out his ragged clothes as an owl puffs out his feathers ... and fell to the sidewalk like a sun-stricken horse.

(Snuffy "collapses" onto the bench at right. Nurse "enters")

Storyteller 1: When the ambulance came, the doctor and young nurse cursed softly at Snuffy's weight.

Nurse: There was no smell of whiskey to justify a transfer to a patrol wagon.

Storyteller 2: So, Snuffy and his two dinners went to the hospital, where they stretched him out on a bed and began to

Nurse: Test him for gastro-intestinal diseases.

(Mr. Cabot lies on the bench at left)

Storyteller 1: And lo! an hour later, another ambulance brought Mr. Cabot to the same hospital. They laid him out on another bed and asked,

Nurse: Heart attack?

Storyteller 2: Soon, the young nurse met one of the young doctors whose eyes she liked, and stopped to chat with him about the cases.

Nurse: Mr. Cabot, that nice, old gentleman in room 20 — now you wouldn't think it to look at him, but it's a case of near starvation. Proud old family, I guess. *(Pauses)* He told us ... that he hadn't eaten a thing in three days.

The End

Source: A short story by O. Henry, which first appeared in the *New York Sunday World Magazine* on November 26, 1905.

71

Why The Evergreen Trees Never Lose Their Leaves

Cast
Narrator
Bird
Birch Tree
Oak Tree
Willow Tree
Juniper Tree
Pine Tree
Spruce Tree
North Wind
Voice Of God

(The Narrator sits to one side of the stage or playing area. The actors playing the Birch, Oak, and Willow Trees stand on chairs at stage right; the actors playing the Juniper, Pine, and Spruce Trees stand on chairs at stage left. The Bird hobbles among them. It works better if the actor doing the Voice Of God looks upstage, away from the audience)

Narrator: Winter was coming, and the birds had all flown south, where the air is warm and where they could find berries to eat. One little bird, however, had broken its wing and could not fly with the others. It was alone in the cold world of frost and snow. The forest looked warm, so the little bird made its way to the trees, as well as it could, to ask for help. First it came to a birch tree.

Bird: Beautiful birch tree, my wing is broken, and my friends have all flown south for the winter. May I live among your branches until they come back?

Birch: No, indeed! We trees of the great forest have our own birds to help. I can do nothing for you.

73

Bird: Well, the birch is not very strong, and it might be that he [she] could not hold me easily. I will ask the oak. Great oak tree, you are so strong. Will you let me live in your boughs until my friends come back in the spring time?

Oak: In the spring time! That is a long way off. How do I know what you might do in all that time? Birds are always looking for something to eat, and you might eat up some of my acorns.

Narrator: The little bird hobbled on.

Bird: It may be that the willow will be kind to me. Gentle willow, my wing is broken, and I could not fly south with the other birds. May I live on your branches until the spring?

Narrator: The willow did not look so gentle then, for he [she] drew himself [herself] up proudly and said,

Willow: Indeed, I do not know you. We willows never talk to people whom we do not know. Perhaps there are trees somewhere that will take in strange birds.

Narrator: The poor, little bird did not know what to do. It moved as well as it could through the snow. Before it had gone far, it heard a voice.

Spruce: Little bird, where are you going?

Narrator: It was the voice of a spruce tree.

Bird: I do not know. And I am very cold.

Spruce: Come right here, then. You can live among my warmest branches all winter long if you like.

Bird: Will you really let me?

Spruce: Why, of course. If your friends have flown away, it is time for the trees to help you, and my branches are thick and soft.

Narrator: Then the pine tree joined it.

Pine: My branches are not thick, but I am big and strong. I can keep the north wind away from you and the spruce.

Juniper: I can help, too,

Narrator: added the juniper tree.

Juniper: I can give you berries all winter long. Every bird knows that juniper berries are delicious.

Narrator: So the spruce tree gave the lonely little bird a home. The pine tree kept the cold north wind away, and the juniper gave the bird berries to eat. The other trees, however, looked on with scorn.

Birch: I would not have a strange bird in my boughs.

Oak: I would not give my acorns away to anyone.

Willow: I never have anything to do with strangers.

Narrator: And the birch, the oak, and the willow drew their leaves closely about them. *(Birch, Oak, and Willow wrap their arms around themselves.)* But the next morning, all their shiny green leaves lay on the ground, for the cold north wind had come in the night, and every leaf that it touched fell from the tree.

North Wind: May I touch every leaf in the forest?

Narrator: Asked the north wind in its frolic. But God answered,

Voice Of God: No. The trees that have been kind to the little bird with the broken wing may keep their leaves all winter long.

Narrator: That is why the spruce, the pine, and the juniper are always green, and that is why the evergreen tree is the symbol of kindness and of the birth of a new life at Christmastime.

The End

Source: There is a version of this folk tale in *Good Stories for Great Holidays* by Frances Jenkins Olcott, published by Houghton Mifflin Company in 1914.

Million Dollar Christmas

Go, sell what you possess and give to the poor and you will have treasure in heaven.
— Matthew 19:21 (See also Mark 10:21)

Cast
Edgar 1
Edgar 2
Bartimaeus Tintoes
Helene
Essay Reader 1
Essay Reader 2
Essay Reader 3

(Edgar 1 sits facing the audience and addresses the audience only. Edgar 2 stands next to him, but speaks to himself and the other characters in the play. Helene and Essay Readers 1-3 sit at center and stand when they "enter")

Edgar 1: I rubbed my eyes and looked at the letter a second time. Yes, I was not asleep; the thing *had* happened. There was my cup of coffee and the half-eaten donut just as I had left them when I went to get the mail. There was the other letter that had come, still unopened, and here was this one from a firm of lawyers I had never heard of. The sum and substance of it was this — my old neighbor, John Dolby, whose funeral I had just attended two days before, had made me the sole heir of his entire estate, which, to quote the letter before me, "Runs considerably over one million dollars." My first act was to pour the whole pitcher of cream, half of which I was saving for my evening tea, into my coffee. What did it matter? I was a millionaire.

Edgar 2: Well,

Edgar 1: I said to myself,

Edgar 2: I can have anything I want now. I'm a millionaire.

Edgar 1: Then I said to myself,

Edgar 2: What in the world were those things I wanted so much? I remember thinking of them, lately, and wishing I could have them, but knowing I couldn't have them. I will be able to get them now. What in the world were they?

Edgar 1: One by one they began to come back to me. I had wished that my housekeeper Mary's nose might be a half an inch shorter than it was. Another thing was that my sister-in-law would stop her exaggerated boasting about her quite average children. And, oh yes, I remembered another thing I had often said to myself that I desired more than anything in the world: that my sister Jane might have a sense of humor. Well, I am a millionaire now and can have anything I wanted.

Edgar 2: I will have these things attended to right off.

Edgar 1: Suddenly, it struck me with a cold shock that, after all, I was no better off than I was before. A million dollars might shorten Mary's nose, but it wouldn't go any way at all toward correcting that annoying trait in my brother's wife or giving Jane a sense of humor. *(Pause)* Nor would it help in the winning of the other thing which, if the truth be told, I desired more than any of these.

Edgar 2: No.

Edgar 1: I sadly thought,

Edgar 2: Even the possession of a million dollars will not make me appear a whit more attractive or desirable in the eyes of a woman who seems to regard me, as far as I can ascertain, as a mere object in her landscape.

Edgar 1: The fact was that the million did not seem to help me get the things I wanted most after all. Money tends to cushion you up among things and it was people that I was most interested in. After all, what did I want with a million?

Edgar 2: One thing is clear. I'll give this million away and be done with it at the first opportunity.

Edgar 1: I said this to myself as I picked up and opened the second letter which was lying unopened beside my plate.

Edgar 2: Ah, yes,

Edgar 1: I said as I read it over quickly,

Edgar 2: Here is a chance, right away, to do some good with it.

Edgar 1: This is what the second letter said.

Tintoes: *(Reads letter)*
National Society for the Redemption of Christmas
23 Wall Street, New York

Dear Sir:

A number of public-spirited citizens have banded together for the purpose of redeeming Christmas from the many wasteful and useless features which cluster around it and, instead, transforming it into an annual event which will be of real economic and moral value to the community. In the past, the untrue legend of Santa Claus has deluded children with the expectation of something for nothing. The destruction of thousands of young trees has robbed the future of thousands of dollars worth of pine and spruce lumber. A great amount of money is expended on absolutely useless illuminated cards, Christmas tree ornaments, candles, fancy wrapping paper and ribbon, house decorations, holly, mistletoe, and other such extravagant, and useless, vanities. If the money, which runs to waste in these useless channels, were only put in the savings bank, we calculate that every man, woman, and child in North America would have $2.54 in his bank account on January first.

Still more serious is this matter when we regard it from the point of view of what this money would do in providing practical, useful gifts for those who need them this year. It has been calculated that the amount thus wasted on folderol would purchase one warm flannel night gown for every widow and a pair of shoes for every orphan in our public institutions.

In view of these facts, we ask you to sign and send us the enclosed pledge that you will spend an entirely rational and utilitarian Christmas, spending money only on useful and rational objects.

Sincerely,
Bartimaeus Tintoes, President

Edgar 2: What wonderful luck! To get a million dollars and directions for the most useful way of spending it in the same day.

Edgar 1: The doorbell rang and, in a moment, Mary's nose appeared at the door, followed, after a lapse of a moment, by Mary herself to say that Miss Helene Gracie wished to see me.

Edgar 2: What a morning I'm having!

Edgar 1: All the best things in the world were pouring in upon me — money, directions for spending it ... and now, the very beatific vision herself was at my door. She came in and sat down in the armchair by the fire. She had never been to see me before, but somehow as she sat there, I remembered having seen her in that very chair thousands of times in my daydreams.

Edgar 2: Would you like a donut?

Edgar 1: I handed her the plate. She took one.

Helene: Thank you. I am really quite hungry. I was out skating for an hour and had an early breakfast.

Edgar 2: Take a lot, take two! Don't mind the expense. I'm a millionaire.

Helene: I'm so glad to hear that, because I have come to ask you for a donation.

Edgar 2: I'm sorry, but you couldn't have struck me at a worse time. I have just arranged to give liberally to this cause.

Edgar 1: I handed her the letter from Mr. Bartimaeus Tintoes.

Helene: Oh, I am sorry. I hoped you would give a dollar to help us buy old Mrs. Gulpins a canary and a cage.

Edgar 1: She read the letter without a word or sign, folded it carefully, and then suddenly, leaning forward, threw it into the reddest part of the fire.

Helene: Nonsense!

Edgar 2: Oh, I have the address on the envelope anyway. I suppose you're mad because you know Mr. Tintoes is perfectly right. A canary for Mrs. Gulpins! You know perfectly well that she barely has enough to eat. She needs potatoes and a new winter coat. Now, what you took for a joke is quite true, Helene. Mr. Dolby has made me his heir.

Edgar 1: I handed her the lawyer's letter. She read through it, did not throw it into the fire, and returned it to me.

Helene: Well, I'm afraid that spoils you. No, I won't ask you for even a dollar. You can't afford it, poor man. They've robbed you of all the riches of life and given you instead another man's cast-off clothes. It's all nonsense, this practical business. Mrs. Gulpins wants a canary in a cage. She has been dreaming of having one in her sunny bay window for years, but she's never bought herself one because she thinks it's frivolous. You and I think she ought to have potatoes and a winter coat.

Well, perhaps she should. If so, we ought to see that she gets them some other time of the year, but not on Christmas. All the potatoes and coats in the world wouldn't make her one millionth as happy as this canary she has her heart set on. Christmas is the time to give people the things that will make them happy, not the things they need. Look at my little brother, Tommy. What I think he needs most of all is a good spanking, but Christmas is not the time for giving him that. Instead I'm going to give him the most useless toy telescope you ever saw — because he wants it.

(Pause)

Edgar 2: Well, Helene, since you put it that way, I guess you are right. I'll tell you what ... I made a vow just before you came in. It was to get rid of the entire million before Christmas Day, so as to be able to enjoy myself again. Now I will make a second vow to spend it all on things that may appear frivolous and useless, provided they give real pleasure to the people who get them. I want to blow it all in a great bacchanalia of joy to other folks of the most unexpected, and yet longed-for, luxuries and happiness, and I want you to help me plan the whole thing out. Will you help me if I come around to your house this evening?

Helene: Show me that you are in earnest by giving me that dollar donation.

Edgar 1: I handed it to her.

Edgar 2: Now I have one dollar less to spend on lightening my burden.

Helene: You have more sense than I thought, Edgar. I'll see you this evening.

Edgar 1: That evening, I rang the bell at Helene's door. I found her sitting at the dining room table with a pencil and a blank sheet of paper in front of her. As I came into the room, her face was as blank as the paper.

Edgar 2: Well, Helene, what have you come up with?

Helene: I had no idea it was going to be such work. I sat down excitedly after dinner to spend your million as foolishly as we could and I can't think of a single useless way to spend it that won't do more harm than good. Before I had a fortune, I mean before you had a fortune, to dispose of, I knew lots of ways to spend it. But now I can't think of one.

Edgar 1: We sat at the table, appalled at the situation — blank paper, blank faces, hearts beating blank, blank, blank. Sadly, I began to be convinced of the impossibility of doing any real good with my million. I could increase the brick and mortar of a score of universities, but what those schools needed was more inspirational teachers and more ambitious students, and that my money was powerless to give. I wanted something that would give at least a moment of glorious life to people who had never had the chance to feel that way.

Helene: This won't do. Who are the people who deserve to have fun out of this million? We must write the answer to that question on our papers before the clock strikes nine.

Edgar 2: But, Helene, it's five minutes to nine.

Edgar 1: The wheels in my brain began to buzz.

Edgar 2: Something must be thought of and thought of immediately.

Edgar 1: Three minutes, four minutes passed, and just as the clock was about to strike nine, we both used our pencils simultaneously, and wrote something on our papers. Now you may believe in divine providence, as you please, but the fact remains that both of us had written the same word. And that word was ...

Helene & Edgar 2: Mothers!

Edgar 1: At last we had something to start on. We were agreed that the mothers of the world were the people who denied themselves the things they wanted in order to give to others.

Helene: Ah, ha! I have the whole thing ready now! We get in touch with the teachers in the schools in the poorer neighborhoods and have them assign a theme for the children to write titled, "What Would Mother Like For Christmas?" We will explain that it is not what mother needs, but what she would like. And it is not what mother wants others to have, but what she would like for herself. We will tell the children that there is a good chance that their mothers' wishes will be granted.

Edgar 2: Let's appoint ourselves the judges.

Edgar 1: A week later, we were seated at the same table with a pile of essays in front of us. What a wonderful study they had been. First, there were a great many suggestions in which our fallen human nature had played a part, such as this specimen,

Essay Reader 1: I think the thing that would give my mother the greatest pleasure would be to see me riding around on one of those bicycles that are in the window of Tontine's Department Store. She has often said that she would enjoy that more than anything in the world.

Edgar 1: Some had to be rejected because they suggested things that no money could buy.

Essay Reader 2: That little children who have gone to a better land might come back into their mothers' arms if only for a moment.

Essay Reader 3: The thing my mother would like most would be that my father would be the way he used to be.

Edgar 1: The list of articles suggested included:

Essay Reader 1: Pieces of jewelry,

Essay Reader 2: Silk dresses,

Essay Reader 3: New hats,

Essay Reader 1: Pictures of all kinds,

Essay Reader 2: Chiefly enlarged family photos,

Essay Reader 3: And rocking chairs for the parlor.

Essay Reader 1: My mother wants enough money to print a little book of poems she has written so that she can give copies to her friends.

Essay Reader 2: Money to buy candles to light for my dead brother.

Essay Reader 3: My mother's longing is for rosebud wall paper for the living room.

Essay Reader 1: A season's ticket to the symphony.

Essay Reader 2: Being able to have some big, yellow chrysanthemums on the table every week.

Edgar 1: I chuckled to myself as I thought,

Edgar 2: How enraged Mr. Bartimaeus Tintoes would be to see me writing an order for a set of expensive furs for a Mexican woman who supported her family by cleaning other people's houses. But that was what little Maria said her mother wanted most of all.

Edgar 1: The Mexican woman would probably put them in a box and keep them until the moths ate them, but in the meantime, every morning she woke she would feel the beatitude of the possession of those furs as a kind of "glory in a box" before she slipped out into the dark to wash floors until it grew dark again. It was great fun going over the pile of essays on the table.

Essay Reader 3: My mother would like most of all to see her old home in Poland again and her old mother, who still lives there, but she cannot get anyone to look after us children while's she's away.

Edgar 1: Helene knew how that could be arranged and I wrote out an order for a trip to Poland.

Essay Reader 1: Gold-rimmed glasses instead of steel spectacles.

Essay Reader 2: A piano to put knickknacks on top of.

Essay Reader 3: Mother says what she would like most of all would be to get away from the sound of a baby or any of us children for about a week, so that she could sleep late and sit down once in a while during the daytime.

Edgar 1: Forty-two mothers were given orders for vacations at various longed-for places from Cape Cod to Paris, with the provision made for a trained helper to look after their homes in the meantime. Helene and I spent a series of the most delightful evenings together until the last week before Christmas when I began to total up just how much I had spent.

Edgar 2: Hard to spend a million? Why it's the easiest thing in the world. How the figures mount up! After a while, you begin to appreciate how small a sum of money a million dollars really is.

Edgar 1: Early on Christmas Eve, Helene and I went to bring Mrs. Gulpins the canary and cage she had never expected to see.

(Edgar 2 hums "Silent Night" or another Christmas carol)

Edgar 1: As we walked home, house after house was illuminated and the sounds of the greatest joy often came out of the small houses. There were tears in both our eyes.

Edgar 2: Well, I don't think that a million dollars ever gave so much pleasure before, do you?

Helene: No, it has given at least one moment of glorious life to the very mothers who thought their lives were doomed to drabness. There is one thing I regret, though. You have spent fifty dollars more than your million and you haven't bought a single thing for yourself. I wish I had asked Mary, your housekeeper, what luxury you would like.

(Pause)

Edgar 2: Well, Helene, since you mentioned it, I'll tell you exactly what I want most, and it fits into our plan perfectly because it is something very ornamental indeed.

Edgar 1: We were coming in under the trees in front of her house. I took my life into my hands and told her just exactly what I wanted for Christmas more than anything else in the world.

(Edgar 2 whisper's into Helene's ear and she whispers something back)

Edgar 1: And do you know what? ... I got it.

Helene: Merry Christmas, Edgar. *(Kisses Edgar 2)*

The End

Source: *How I Spent My Million* by Rev. J. Edgar Park, published by Pilgrim Press, Boston in 1913.

The Burglar's Christmas

But the father said to his servants, "Bring quickly the best robe and put it on him; and put a ring on his hand, and shoes on his feet, and bring the fatted calf and kill it, and let us eat and make merry; for this son of mine was dead and is alive again; he was lost and is found."
— Luke 15:22-24

This play, based on a short story by Willa Cather, is an allegorical retelling of the story of the prodigal son told from the perspective of the mother, rather than of the father.

Cast
Narrator 1
Narrator 2
Young Man
Will
Mother
Father

(Narrators are seated on stools or chairs at stage right and stage left. Mother and Father are sitting on a bench or chairs up stage facing away from the audience. There is an unoccupied chair or stool in center stage. Will and Young Man are standing at center stage slightly down from the unoccupied chair)

Narrator 1: Two very shabby-looking young men stood at the corner, looking despondently at the carriages that whirled by.

Narrator 2: It was Christmas Eve, and the streets were in that half-liquid, half-congealed condition peculiar to the streets of Chicago at that season of the year.

Young Man: Well, I guess we are at our rope's end, sure enough. How do you feel?

Will: Pretty shaky. The wind's sharp tonight. If I had anything to eat, I wouldn't mind it so much. There is just no use. I'm sick of the whole business. Looks like there's nothing left for me but Lake Michigan.

Young Man: Oh, nonsense, I thought you had more grit than that. Got anything left you can pawn?

Will: Nothing but my beard, and I am afraid they wouldn't find it worth a pawn ticket.

Young Man: Got any folks anywhere? Now's the time to put the bite on 'em if you have.

Will: Never mind if I have, they're out of the question.

Young Man: Well, you'll be out of it before long if you don't make a move of some sort. A man's got to eat. See here, I am going down to Longtin's saloon. I used to play the banjo in there and I'll squeeze him for some of his free-lunch stuff. You'd better come along. Perhaps, they'll fill an order for two.

Will: How far down is it?

Young Man: Well it's clear downtown, of course, way down on Michigan Avenue.

Will: Thanks, I guess I'll loaf around here. I don't feel equal to the walk, and the cars — well, the cars are crowded.

Young Man: No, you never did like streetcars, you're too aristocratic. See here, Crawford, I don't like leaving you here. You ain't good company for yourself tonight.

Will: Crawford? Oh, yes, that's the last one. I've had so many names I forget them.

Young Man: Have you even got a real name, anyway?

Will: Oh, yes, but it's one of the ones I've forgotten. Don't you worry about me. You go along and get your free lunch. I think I had a fight in Longtin's place once. I'd better not show myself there again.

(Young Man exits)

Narrator 1: He was miserable enough to want to be quite alone. He wanted to think about himself. He had avoided this final reckoning with himself for a year now. He had laughed it off and drunk it off.

Will: Hunger is a powerful incentive to introspection. It is a tragic hour, that hour when we are finally driven to reckon with ourselves, when every avenue of mental distraction has been cut off and our own life and all its failures closes about us like the walls of an old torture chamber.

(Narrators stand and move slightly behind and to the left and right of Will. In the following speeches, they speak directly to him as if they are the voices of his thoughts. Will turns up his collar and tries to stay warm during their speeches)

Narrator 2: Tonight, as this man stood stranded in the streets of the city, his hour came. It was not the first time he had been hungry and desperate and alone.

Will: But always before there was some outlook, some chance ahead, some pleasure yet untasted, that seemed worth the effort, some face that I fancied was, or would be, dear.

91

Narrator 2: But it was not so tonight. The unyielding conviction was upon him now that he had failed in everything, had outlived everything.

Narrator 1: It had been near him for a long time, that Pale Specter. He had caught its shadow at the bottom of his glass many a time. It had made life hateful to him when he awoke in the morning, before now. Now it settled slowly over him, like night.

Narrator 1: Yet, he was but four and twenty, this man — he looked even younger — and he had a father some place back East who had been very proud of him once.

Will: Well, I have taken my life into my own hands, and this is what I have made of it.

Narrator 2: As he stood there in the wet under the streetlight, he drew up his reckoning with the world and decided that it had treated him as well as he deserved. He had overdrawn his account once too often.

Will: There was a day when I thought otherwise, when I said I was unjustly handled, that my failure was merely the lack of proper adjustment between myself and other people, that some day I would be recognized and it would all come right.

Narrator 2: But he knew better than that now, and he was still man enough to bear no grudge against anyone.

Narrator 1: Tonight was his birthday, too. He instinctively began to remember all the birthday parties he used to have. He was so cold and empty that his mind seemed unable to grapple with any serious questions. He kept thinking about gingerbread and frosted cakes, like a child.

(Narrators return to their stools)

Will: I can still remember the splendid birthday parties my mother used to give me, when all the other boys on the block came in their Sunday clothes and creaking shoes, with their ears still red from their mother's towel. And the pink and white birthday cake, and all the dishes that I was particularly fond of, and how I would eat and eat and then go to bed and dream of Santa Claus. In the morning I would awaken and eat again, until by night the family doctor arrived with his castor oil. I used to dolefully say that it was altogether too much to have your birthday and Christmas all at once. I can remember, too, the royal birthday dinners I had given at college, and the toasts, and the music, and the good fellows who had wished me happiness and really meant what they said.

Narrator 2: Whichever way his mind now turned, there was one thought that it could not escape, and that was the idea of food. He felt a sharp pain in the pit of his stomach. For a moment, he felt that bitter hatred of wealth, of ease, of everything that is well fed and well housed that is common to starving men.

Will: At any rate, I have a right to eat!

Narrator 2: He had demanded great things from the world once: fame and wealth and admiration. Now it was simply bread — and he would have it!

Narrator 1: In all his straits he had never stolen anything; his tastes were above it. But tonight there would be no tomorrow. He had failed at everything else, now he would see what his chances would be as a common thief. It would be interesting to add another study to his gallery of futile attempts, and then label them all:

Will: Failure as a journalist. Failure as a lecturer. Failure as a businessman. Failure as a thief.

Narrator 1: A carriage then drove up to the house before which he stood. Several richly dressed women alighted and went in.

Will: It's a new house ... must have been built since I was last in Chicago.

(Will takes one or two steps forward as if to see into the house)

Narrator 1: The front door was open and he could see down the hallway and up the staircase. The servant had left the door open and gone with the guests.

Narrator 2: The first floor was brilliantly lighted, but the windows upstairs were dark. It looked very easy just to slip upstairs to the darkened rooms where the jewels and trinkets of the fashionable occupants were kept.

Narrator 1: He entered quickly. His way was clear enough; he met no one on the stairway or in the upper hall. He passed the first door through sheer cowardice.

Narrator 2: The second he entered quickly, thinking of something else lest his courage should fail him, and closed the door behind him.

Narrator 1: The room was furnished richly enough to justify his expectations. He went at once to the dressing case. A number of rings and small trinkets lay in a silver tray. These he put hastily in his pocket.

Narrator 2: He opened the upper drawer and found, as he expected, several leather cases. In the first that he opened was a lady's watch, in the second a pair of old-fashioned bracelets. He seemed to dimly remember

Will: having seen bracelets like them before, somewhere.

Narrator 1: The third case was heavier, the spring was much worn, and it opened easily. It held a cup of some kind. He held it up to the light and then his strained nerves gave way.

(Will utters a sharp, painful exclamation)

Narrator 2: It was the silver mug he used to drink from when he was a little boy.

(Mother enters)

Narrator 1: The door opened, and a woman stood in the doorway facing him. The light from the hall streamed in upon him, but she was not afraid.

Mother: Willie, Willie! Is that you?

Narrator 2: He struggled to loosen her arms from him, to keep her lips from his cheek.

Will: Mother — you mustn't! You don't understand! Oh my God, this is worst thing possible!

Narrator 2: Hunger, weakness, cold, shame, all came back to him, and shook his self-control completely. Physically, he was too weak to stand a shock like this.

Will: *(To audience)* Why could it not have been an ordinary discovery, arrest, the police station, and all the rest of it? Anything but this!

Mother: Who says I can't kiss my own son? Oh, my boy, we have waited so long for this! You have been so long in coming back that even I almost gave up.

Will: You don't understand. I didn't know you lived here. I came here to rob. It is the first time — I swear it — but I am a common thief. My pockets are full of your jewels now. Don't you understand? I'm a common thief!

Mother: Hush. My boy, those are ugly words. How could you rob your own house? How could you take what is your own? They are all yours, son, as wholly yours as my love — and you can't doubt that, Will, do you?

Narrator 1: That soft voice, the warmth, and fragrance of her person stole through his chilly, empty veins like a gentle stimulant.

Will: Oh, Mother, life is hard, hard!

Narrator 2: For a moment they stood silently. Then they heard a heavy step upon the stair. She went out and closed the door. At the top of the staircase she met a tall, broad-shouldered man, with iron-gray hair, and a face alert and stern.

(Father enters)

Mother: James, it is William in there, come home. You must keep him at any cost. If he goes this time, I go with him. Oh, James, be easy with him, he has suffered so.

Father: You go to him now, he will stay. I will go to my room. I will see him in the morning.

Mother: Oh, James, I thank you, I thank you! This is the night he came so long ago, you remember? I gave him to you then, and now give him back to me!

Father: Don't Helen. He is my son, too; I have never forgotten that. I failed with him. I don't like to fail, it cuts my pride.

(Father exits)

Narrator 2: She flew into the room where the young man stood with his head bowed.

Mother: He is so glad, Willie, so glad! He may not show it, but he is as happy as I am. He never was demonstrative with either of us, you know.

Will: Oh my God, he was good enough. I don't see how either of you can look at me, speak to me, touch me.

Mother: This is my right, my son ... Now come with me into the library, and I will have your dinner brought there. I will not call your sister Ellen tonight; she has a number of guests to attend to. She is big girl now, you know. Besides, I want you all to myself tonight.

Narrator 1: When the dinner came, he fell upon it savagely. As he ate, she told him all that had transpired during the years of his absence, and how his father's business had brought them there.

Mother: I was glad when we came to Chicago, because I thought you would drift west. I seemed a good deal nearer to you here.... Have you everything you want? It is a comfort to see you eat.

Will: It's certainly a comfort to me. I have not indulged in this frivolous habit for some 36 hours.

Mother: Don't say that! I know it, but I can't bear to hear you say it — it's too terrible! My boy, food has choked me many a time when I have thought of the possibility of that. Now, take the old lounge chair by the fire, and if you are too tired to talk, we will just sit and rest together. *(Will sits on the stool in center stage)*

Narrator 2: He sank into the depths of the big leather chair with the lions' heads on the arms, where he had sat so often in the days when his feet did not touch the floor. He felt

Will: *(To audience)* a sudden yearning tenderness for the happy little boy who sat there and dreamed of the big world, so long ago. Alas, he has been dead many a summer, that little boy!

Narrator 1: He sat looking up at the magnificent woman beside him. Then, in the deep red coals of the grate, he saw the faces of other women who had come, since then, into his vexed, disordered life.

Will: *(To audience)* Laughing faces, with eyes, artificially bright eyes, without depth or meaning.

Will: *(To Mother)* Ah, Mother, you make other things seem so false. You must feel that I owe you an explanation, but I can't make any, even to myself. We make poor exchanges in life. I can't make out the riddle of it all. Yet, there are things I ought to tell you before I accept your confidence like this.

Mother: I'd rather you wouldn't, Will. Listen, between you and me there can be no secrets. This is your birthday night. From the hour you were born, you were restless and discontented. You used to brace your strong little limbs against mine and try to throw me off, as you did tonight. Tonight, you have come back to me, just as you always did after you ran away to swim in the river that was forbidden you, the river you loved because it was forbidden. You are tired and sleepy, just as you used to be then, only a little older and a little paler and a little more foolish. I never asked you where you had been then, nor will I now. You have come back to me, that's all in all to me.

Will: I wonder if you know just how much you pardon?

Mother: Oh, my poor Willie, much or little, what does it matter? Have you wandered so far and paid such a bitter price for knowledge and not yet learned that love has nothing to do with pardon or forgiveness, that it only loves, and loves — and loves? They have not taught you well, the women of your world.

Narrator 2: She leaned over and kissed him, as no woman had kissed him since he left her. He drew a long sigh of rich contentment. The old life, with all its bitterness and useless antagonism, seemed distant and far away.

Narrator 1: And as the chimes rang joyfully outside, and sleep pressed heavily upon his eyelids, he wondered dimly if the Grand Author of this sad little riddle of ours we call life might not be able to solve it after all.

The End

Source: *The Burglar's Christmas* by Willa Cather (c1876-1947) was first published in *Home Monthly* magazine in December, 1896.

Christmas Every Day

Cast
Storyteller 1
Storyteller 2
Little Girl
Everybody — plays the Christmas fairy, the other children, Mother, Father, the police, and so on. (If the director wants to use more actors, he or she can divide this into two or three roles. However, it works very well if one actor does all the roles and changes voices.)

(The actors are standing or seated from stage right to stage left: Storyteller 1, Little Girl, Everybody, and Storyteller 2)

Storyteller 1: Once there was a little girl who liked Christmas so much she wanted it

Little Girl: to be Christmas every day in the year.

Storyteller 1: And as soon as Thanksgiving was over, she began to send postcards to the old Christmas fairy to ask if she might not have it.

Storyteller 2: But the old fairy never answered any of the postcards, and after a while, the little girl found out that the fairy was

Little Girl: pretty particular

Storyteller 2: and wouldn't even notice anything

Little Girl: but real letters on sheets of paper, and sealed outside with a monogram — or your initial, anyway.

Storyteller 1: So then she began to send her letters, and in about three weeks — or just the day before Christmas — she got a letter from the fairy saying,

Everybody: you may have Christmas every day for a year, and then we will see about having it longer.

Storyteller 2: The little girl was a good deal excited already, preparing for the old-fashioned, once-a-year Christmas that was coming the next day, and perhaps the fairy's promise didn't make such an impression on her as it would have made at some other time. She just resolved to keep it to herself,

Little Girl: and surprise everybody with it as it kept coming true.

Storyteller 2: Then it slipped out of her mind altogether.

Storyteller 1: She had a splendid Christmas. She went to bed early,

Little Girl: so as to let Santa Claus have a chance at the stockings.

Storyteller 1: In the morning she was up the first of anybody and went and felt the stockings, and found hers

Little Girl: all lumpy with packages of candy, and oranges and grapes, and pocketbooks and rubber balls, and all kinds of small presents,

Storyteller 1: just as she always had every Christmas.

Storyteller 2: Then she waited around until the rest of the family was up, and she was the first to burst into the living room, when the doors were opened, and look at the large presents laid out on the floor.

Little Girl: Books and boxes of stationery, and dolls and little stoves and dozens of handkerchiefs and skates and snow shovels and photograph frames and boxes of watercolors and candied cherries and dolls' houses and a sled — and the big Christmas tree, lighted and standing in the middle.

Storyteller 1: She had a splendid Christmas all day. She ate so much candy that she did not want any breakfast, and the whole afternoon, the presents kept pouring in. She went around giving the presents she had for other people, and came home

Little Girl: and ate turkey and cranberries for dinner, and plum pudding and nuts and raisins and oranges ... and more candy.

Storyteller 1: Then she went out and coasted on her new sled and came in with a stomachache, crying. They had a light supper, and pretty early everybody went to bed, cross.

Storyteller 2: The little girl slept very heavily, and she slept very late, but she was wakened at last by the other children dancing around her bed with their stockings full of presents in their hands.

Little Girl: What is it?

Storyteller 1: said the little girl, and she rubbed her eyes and tried to rise up in bed.

Everybody: Christmas! Christmas! Christmas!

Storyteller 1: They all shouted, and waved their stockings.

Little Girl: Nonsense! It was Christmas yesterday.

Storyteller 1: Her brothers and sisters just laughed.

Everybody: We don't know about that. It's Christmas today, anyway. You come into the living room and see.

Storyteller 2: Then, all at once, it flashed on the little girl

Little Girl: that the fairy was keeping her promise,

Storyteller 2: and her year of Christmases was beginning. She was dreadfully sleepy, but she sprang up like a lark — a lark that had overeaten itself and gone to bed cross — and darted into the living room. There it was again!

Little Girl: Books and dolls and boxes of stationery and the Christmas tree blazing away, and the family picking out their presents, but looking pretty sleepy, and father perfectly puzzled, with mother ready to cry.

Everybody: I'm sure I don't see how I'm to dispose of all these things,

Storyteller 1: said her mother; and her father said,

Everybody: It seems to me we had something just like this yesterday, but I suppose I must have dreamed it.

Storyteller 1: The next day, it was just the same thing over again, but everybody was getting more cross. At the end of a week's time, so many people had lost their tempers that you could pick up lost tempers everywhere; they perfectly strewed the ground. Even when people tried to recover their tempers, they usually got somebody else's, and made the most dreadful mix.

Storyteller 2: The little girl began to get frightened, keeping the secret all to herself. She wanted to tell her mother, but she didn't dare to; and she was ashamed to ask the fairy to take back her gift, it seemed

Little Girl: ungrateful and ill-mannered.

Storyteller 2: She thought she would try to stand it, but she hardly knew how she could, for a whole year.

Little Girl: So it went on and on, and it was Christmas on Saint Valentine's Day and Washington's Birthday just the same as any day.

Storyteller 2: Fourth of July speeches all turned into Christmas carols.

Storyteller 1: After a while, turkeys became so scarce they got to be

Little Girl: about $1,000 apiece!

Storyteller 1: They began passing off almost anything for turkeys. And cranberries — well, they asked

Everybody: *(Holding up an imaginary cranberry and calling like a street vendor)* a diamond apiece for cranberries!

Storyteller 2: All the woods and orchards were cut down for Christmas trees, and where the woods and orchards used to be, it looked just like a stubble-field, with the stumps.

Storyteller 1: After a while, they had to make Christmas trees out of rags and stuff them with bran, like old-fashioned dolls; but there were plenty of rags, because people got so poor buying presents for one another that they couldn't get any new clothes, and they just wore their old ones to tatters.

Everybody: *(Hoarsely)* Some people lost their voices from saying, "Merry Christmas" so much.

Storyteller 2: After it had gone on about five or six months, the little girl, whenever she came into the room in the morning and saw

Little Girl: those great, ugly lumpy stockings dangling at the fireplace, and the disgusting presents around everywhere,

Storyteller 2: used to just sit down and burst out crying. In eight months, she was perfectly exhausted; she couldn't even cry anymore; she just lay on the couch and rolled her eyes and panted.

Storyteller 1: About the beginning of October, she took to sitting down on dolls wherever she found them —

Little Girl: French dolls, or any kind.

Storyteller 1: She hated the sight of them so; and by Thanksgiving, she was crazy and just slammed her presents across the room.

Storyteller 2: By that time, people didn't carry presents around nicely anymore. They'd fling them over the fence, or through the window, or anything, and instead of taking great pains to write

Everybody: *(Sweetly)* For dear Papa or Mama or Brother or Sister or Susie or Sammie or Billie or Bobby or Jimmie or Jennie,

Storyteller 2: or whoever it was, and troubling to get the spelling right, and then signing their names and Merry Christmas — they used to write in the gift books,

Everybody: *(Sourly)* Take it, you horrible old thing!

Storyteller 2: and then go and bang it against the front door.

Storyteller 1: Nearly everybody had built barns to hold their presents, but pretty soon the barns overflowed, and then they used to let the presents lie out in the rain, or anywhere. Sometimes the police used to come and tell them,

Everybody: *(Loudly)* Shovel those presents off the sidewalk or we will arrest you!

Storyteller 2: Well, before it came Thanksgiving, it had leaked out who had caused all these Christmases. The little girl had suffered so much that she had talked about it in her sleep, and after that, hardly anybody would play with her. People just perfectly despised her, because if it had not been for her greediness, it couldn't have happened.

Storyteller 1: So now, when it came Thanksgiving, and she wanted

Little Girl: to go to church, and have a squash pie and turkey, and show gratitude;

Storyteller 1: they said,

Everybody: all the turkeys have been eaten up for your old Christmas dinners,

Storyteller 1: and if she would stop the Christmases, they would see about the gratitude.

Storyteller 2: The very next day, the little girl began to send letters to the Christmas fairy, and then telegrams, to stop it. But it didn't do any good; and then she began calling at the fairy's house, but the girl who came to the door always said,

Everybody: not at home,

Storyteller 2: or

Everybody: engaged,

Storyteller 2: or

Everybody: at dinner,

Storyteller 2: or something like that; and so it went on until it came to the old once-a-year Christmas Eve. The little girl fell asleep, and when she woke up in the morning — *(Pause)*

Storyteller 1: It wasn't Christmas! There was the greatest rejoicing all over the country, and it extended clear up into Canada. The people met together everywhere, and kissed and cried for joy.

Storyteller 2: In the city, carts went around and gathered up all the candy and raisins and nuts and dumped them into the river. It made the fish perfectly sick. The whole United States and Canada, as far out as Alaska, was one blaze of bonfires, where the children were burning up their presents of all kinds. They had the greatest time!

Storyteller 1: The little girl went to thank the old fairy

Little Girl: because she had stopped it being Christmas,

Storyteller 1: and she said she hoped

Little Girl: she would keep her promise and see that Christmas never, never came again.

Storyteller 2: Then the fairy frowned and asked her,

Everybody: Are you sure you know what you mean?

Little Girl: Why not?

Storyteller 2: And the old fairy said,

Everybody: Now you are behaving just as greedily as ever, and you'd better look out.

Storyteller 1: This made the little girl think it all over carefully again, and she said that she

Little Girl: would be willing to have Christmas about once in 1,000 years.

Storyteller 1: And then she said,

Little Girl: 100.

Storyteller 1: And then she said,

Little Girl: ten.

Storyteller 1: And, at last, she got down to

Little Girl: one.

Storyteller 1: Then the fairy said

Everybody: That is the good, old way that has pleased people ever since Christmas began.

Storyteller 2: And the little girl agreed and skipped off, and hippity-hopped the whole way home, she was so glad.

The End

Source: "Christmas Every Day" by William Dean Howells first appeared in *St. Nicholas*, a children's magazine, in January, 1886.

Hoodoo McFiggin's Christmas

Cast
Narrator
Hoodoo McFiggin

(Narrator stands, Hoodoo is sitting)

Narrator: This Santa Claus business is played out. It's a sneaking, underhanded method, and the sooner it's exposed, the better. I had a good opportunity of observing how the thing worked this Christmas, in the case of young Hoodoo McFiggin.

Hoodoo McFiggin is a good boy, a religious boy. He had been given to understand that Santa Claus would bring nothing to his father and mother because grown-up people don't get presents from the angels. So, he saved up all his pocket money and bought a box of cigars for his father and a 75-cent diamond brooch for his mother. His own fortunes, he left in the hands of the angels. But he prayed. He prayed every night for weeks that Santa Claus would bring him

Hoodoo: a pair of skates and a puppy-dog and an air-gun and a bicycle and a Noah's ark and a sleigh and a drum —

Narrator: altogether, about $150 worth of stuff. I peeked into Hoodoo's room quite early Christmas morning. I had an idea that the scene would be interesting. He sat up in bed, his eyes glistening with radiant expectation, and began hauling things out of his stocking.

The first parcel was bulky; it was done up quite loosely and had an odd look generally.

Hoodoo: Ha! Ha!

Narrator: Hoodoo cried gleefully, as he began undoing it.

111

Hoodoo: I'll bet it's the puppy-dog, all wrapped up in paper!

Narrator: And was it the puppy-dog? No, by no means, it was a ... pair of nice, strong, size-four boots, laces and all, labeled,

Hoodoo: To Hoodoo, from Santa Claus.

Narrator: The boy's jaw fell with delight.

Hoodoo: It's boots,

Narrator: he said, and plunged in his hand again. He began hauling away at another parcel with renewed hope on his face. This time the thing seemed like a little round box. Hoodoo tore the paper off it with a feverish hand. He shook it; something rattled inside.

Hoodoo: It's a watch and chain! It's a watch and chain!

Narrator: he shouted. Then he pulled the lid off. And was it a watch and chain? No. It was a box of nice, brand-new ... celluloid collars,

Hoodoo: a dozen of them all alike,

Narrator: and all his own size. The boy was so pleased that you could see his face crack up with pleasure. He waited a few minutes until his intense joy subsided. Then he tried again. This time, the package was long and hard. It resisted the touch and had a sort of funnel shape.

Hoodoo: It's a toy pistol!

Narrator: said the boy, trembling with excitement.

Hoodoo: Gee! I hope there are lots of caps with it! I'll fire some off now and wake up father.

Narrator: No, my poor child, you will not wake your father with that. It is a useful thing, but it needs no caps and it fires no bullets, and you cannot wake a sleeping man with ... a toothbrush. Yes, it was a toothbrush, a regular beauty, pure bone all through, and ticketed with a little paper,

Hoodoo: To Hoodoo, from Santa Claus.

Narrator: Again, the expression of intense joy passed over the boy's face, and the tears of gratitude started from this eyes. He wiped them away with his toothbrush and passed on. The next packet was much larger and evidently contained something soft and bulky. It had been too long to go into the stocking and was tied outside.

Hoodoo: I wonder what this is,

Narrator: Hoodoo mused, half afraid to open it. Then his heart gave a great leap, and he forgot all his other presents in the anticipation of this one.

Hoodoo: It's the drum! It's the drum, all wrapped up!

Narrator: Drum nothing! It was ... pants — a pair of the nicest little short pants — yellowish-brown short pants — with dear little stripes of color running across both ways, and here again, Santa Claus had written,

Hoodoo: To Hoodoo, from Santa Claus.

Narrator: But, there was something wrapped up in it. Oh, yes! There was a pair of suspenders wrapped up in it; suspenders with a little steel sliding thing so that you could slide your pants up to your neck, if you wanted to. The boy gave a dry sob of satisfaction. Then he took out his last present.

Hoodoo: It's a book,

Narrator: he said, as he unwrapped it.

113

Hoodoo: I wonder if it is fairy stories or adventures. Oh, I hope it's adventures! I'll read it all morning.

Narrator: No, Hoodoo, it was not precisely adventures. It was a small ... family Bible. Hoodoo had now seen all his presents, and he arose and dressed. But he still had the fun of playing with his toys.

Hoodoo: That is always the chief delight of Christmas morning.

Narrator: First, he played with his toothbrush. He got a whole lot of water and brushed all his teeth with it. This was huge. Then, he played with his collars. He had no end of fun with them, taking them all out, one-by-one, and swearing at them, and then putting them back and swearing at the whole lot together.

The next toy was his pants. He had immense fun there, putting them on and taking them off again, and then trying to guess which side was which by merely looking at them.

After that he took his book and read some adventures

Hoodoo: called "Genesis"

Narrator: until breakfast time. Then he went downstairs and kissed his father and mother. His father was smoking a cigar, and his mother had her new brooch on. Hoodoo's face was thoughtful, and a light seemed to have broken in upon his mind. Indeed, I think it altogether likely that next Christmas ...

Hoodoo: I will hang onto my money ... and take my chances with what the angels bring.

The End

Source: "Hoodoo McFiggin's Christmas" by Stephen Leacock (1869-1944) is from his collection, *Literary Lapses*, New York: McClelland and Stewart, 1910.

Home For The Holidays

Cast
Narrator
Mother
Father
Arthur
Relatives 1-4

(Narrator is seated at stage right, Arthur stands in the center, Mother and Father are standing stage left. The Relatives 1-4 are seated upstage, away from the audience, until they "enter")

Narrator: To that element of our population that is under the age of 22, these are called, "The Holidays." This is the only chance that the janitors of the colleges have to clean the floors of the classrooms, and while this is being done, there is nothing to do with the students, but to send them home for a week or two. Thus, it happens that the term "holidays" is applied to that period of the year

Father: when everybody else is working twice as hard and twice as long.

Narrator: For those who are home from college it is called, in the catalogs of their institutions,

Arthur: a "recess" or "vacation."

Narrator: And the general impression is allowed to get abroad among the parents

Father: that it is a period of rest and recuperation.

Narrator: Arthur has been working so hard at college,

Mother: that two weeks of good, quiet home life and home cooking will put him right on his feet again,

Narrator: ready to pitch into that chemistry course in which,

Arthur: owing to an incompetent instructor,

Narrator: he did not do very well last term.

That the theory of rest during the vacation is fallacious can be proven by hiding in the clothes-closet of the home of any college youth home for Christmas recess.

Once hidden among the coats and galoshes, you will overhear the following — There is a banging on the door *(Arthur bangs on the side of his book)* and

Father: Arthur has arrived!

(Mother and Father cross to center and stand to the left of Arthur)

Narrator: A round of kisses *(Cast makes kissing sounds)*, an exchange of health reports, and Arthur is bounding upstairs.

Mother: Dinner in half an hour,

Narrator: says Mother.

Arthur: *(Loudly)* Sorry,

Narrator: shouts Arthur from the bathroom.

Arthur: Tom Whortleberry's parents are taking us to their club for dinner. They asked me last week. Say, have I got any cuff links at home? Mine are at school.

Narrator: Father's cuff links are requisitioned and the family clusters at Arthur's door to slide in a few conversational phrases while he is getting into his dress shirt.

Mother: *(As if shouting through the door)* How have you been?

Arthur: Oh, all right. Say, have I got any dress shoes at home? My good ones are at school. Where are the old ones I had last summer?

Father: Do you want me to tie your tie?

Arthur: No, thanks. Can I get my laundry done by tomorrow night? I've got to go to Jim Clamps' in Short Neck for a party, and when I get back from there, I'm supposed to go to the movies with Jane Dibble.

Mother: Don't you want to eat a little something before you go to the Whortleberrys?

(Arthur takes a couple of steps back)

Narrator: But Arthur has bounded down the stairs and left the family to comfort each other with such observations as —

Mother: He looks tired.

Father: I think that he has filled out a little.

Mother: I wonder if he's studying too hard.

Narrator: You might stay in the closet for the entire two weeks and not hear much more of Arthur than this. His parents don't. They catch him

Father: as he is going up and down the stairs,

Mother: and when he picks up his laundry,

Father: and are thankful for that.

Narrator: They really keep in closer touch with him while he is at college,

Mother: for he writes a weekly letter then.

Narrator: Nerve-racking as this sort of life is to the youth who is supposed to be resting during his Christmas vacation, it might be even more wearing if he were to stay within the family precincts. Once in a while, one of the parties falls through and he is

Arthur: *(Pained)* forced to spend an evening at home.

(Arthur steps forward)

Narrator: At first, it is somewhat embarrassing to be thrown in with strangers for a meal like that, but, as the evening wears on, the ice is broken and things assume a more easy swing.

Arthur: *(Pained)* The family begins to make remarks.

Father: You must stand up straighter, my boy. You are slouching badly. I noticed it as you walked down the street this morning.

Mother: Do all the boys wear shirts like that? Personally, I think that they look very untidy. They are all right for sports and things like that, but I wish you'd put on a shirt with a collar when you are in the house. You never see Elmer Quiggly wearing a shirt like that. He always looks neat.

Father: Where did you get that necktie? It looks like a Masonic apron. Let me go with you when you buy your next one.

Narrator: By this time Arthur has his back against the wall and is breathing hard.

Arthur: What do these folks know about what kids are wearing anyway?

Narrator: If it is not family heckling, it may be that even more insidious trial, the third degree. This is usually inflicted by relatives and neighbors.

(Relatives 1-4 come forward and stand close to one another and to Arthur at his right. They speak their lines in rapid succession)

Relative 1: Well, how do you like school?

Relative 2: Do you know a fellow named Spencer Mellish?

Relative 3: What's the matter with the football team this year?

Relative 4: Are you a senior already?

Relative 2: What's your major?

Relative 3: What are you planning to do after college?

Relative 4: Going to college is certainly a lot easier than having to work, isn't it?

Relative 1: I can remember you when you were that high, and used to come over to my house wearing a little green dress with big mother-of-pearl buttons. You certainly were a cute little boy, and used to call me, "Sna-Sna."

(Relatives return upstage)

Narrator: After an hour or so of this, Arthur is willing to go back to college early.

Arthur: And take an extra course in blacksmithing given during the Christmas vacation.

Narrator: And whichever way you look at it, whether he spends his time changing clothes and going off to social functions,

119

Arthur: or goes crazy answering questions and defending my mode of dress,

Narrator: it all adds up to the same in the end — fatigue and

Arthur: a general run-down nervous condition.

Narrator: Which leads me to the conclusion that our educational system is wrong. It is obvious that the young person should be kept at home for nine months of the year and sent to school for the vacations.

The End

Source: "Home for the Holidays" by Robert Benchley appeared in his collection, *Love Conquers All*, published by Henry Holt (New York) in 1922.

Appendix:
Additional Sources For
Christmas Readers' Theater Scripts

A Child is Born by Stephen Vincent Benet. Originally written as a half-hour radio drama for NBC in 1940, this story, set in the inn at Bethlehem, became so popular that it was rebroadcast for many years. It originally starred Broadway actors Alfred Lunt and Lynn Fontaine as the innkeeper and his wife. It can be a very effective staged reading. Baker's Plays / requires payment of a small royalty fee.

A Christmas Carol, adapted by Paul Caywood from the story by Charles Dickens. This concise readers' theater version runs only 45 minutes and requires only eight actors. Meriwether Publishing.

Christmas Comes But Once a Year, compiled by Melvin R. White from Bible quotes, literary selections, and historical extracts. This compendium contains both religious and secular elements and can be expanded or shortened as desired. Meriwether Publishing.

Christmas on Stage, edited by Theodore O. Zapel. This collection contains 27 short Christmas plays, several of which can be done as readers' theater pieces. Meriwether Publishing.

The Christmas Truce by Aaron Shepard. A twelve-minute play for four readers/actors based on the true story of the remarkable, spontaneous, and unofficial truce that took place during Christmas 1914 on the Western Front in World War I. Shepard used excerpts from actual letters and diaries. Available free from his website: www.aaronshep.com.

Gargoyles, Plastic Balls, and Soup by Jack Kurtz. This small volume contains three plays for readers' theater: "Christmas and the Gargoyle Who Couldn't Say No," "Tommy and the Pitiful Pink Plastic Ball," and "Susie and the Christmas Soup." These plays were originally performed as children's sermons so they can easily be staged in a church chancel. All three are humorous with a clear Christian message that will appeal to both adults and children. Baker's Plays / requires payment of a small royalty fee.

The Voices of Christmas by Jerry Nordstrom. This contemporary, humorous script with a subtle Christian message requires nine actors. CSS Publishing.

Baker's Plays
P. O. Box 699222
Quincy, Massachusetts 02269-9222
(617) 745-0805
www.bakersplays.com

CSS Publishing Company
517 South Main Street
Lima, Ohio 45804
(800) 421-4056
www.csspub.com

Lillenas Publishing
P. O. Box 419527
Kansas City, Missouri 64141
(816) 931-1900
www.lillenas.com

Meriwether Publishing
885 Elkton Drive
Colorado Springs, Colorado 80907
(800) 937-5297
www.meriwetherpublishing.com

National Textbook Company
(now part of Glencoe-McGrawHill)
4255 West Touhy Avenue
Lincolnwood, Illinois 60646-1975
(800) 323-4900
www.ntc-school.com